MANGO MAN

By:- Satish Anand

First Published in January 2023

ISBN: 978-93-5668-608-3

BLUEROSE PUBLISHERS

www.BlueRoseONE.com

info@bluerosepublishers.com

+91 8882 898 898

Cover Design:

Satish Anand & Muskan

Typographic Design:

Tanya Raj Upadhyay

Distributed by:

BlueRose, Amazon, Flipkart

For any suggestions mail at: whistleblowersatishanand@gmail.com

About The Poet

"I am a mango man breed,
My sex is unequal equality.
My religion is unknown indeed,
But my caste indicates my ability."

Who is Satish Anand? He is a very simple person like a mango man and he tries his best to peep inside the heart and brain of a common man through his poem "Mango Man." His father, Mr. Ramdeo Pd. Gupta belongs to a rich and prosperous business family whereas his mother, Mrs. Ramawati Gupta is the mayor's daughter whose father, Dr. Kali Prasad, died while she was very young. She had to suffer a lot after marriage as Poet's father couldn't be as successful as his own father. Poet is the fifth and youngest child in his family. After the marriage of poet's two elder sisters and the eldest brother, financial conditions of his family worsened further. It was difficult for the family to support poet's education. He had to take the toughest decision i.e. to leave home. He came to Delhi at a very tender age of mere sixteen for further studies and to earn living. He opted to take tuition classes to keep himself connected with education and earn living. His journey was full of thorns and many a day he had to go without food, but he did not give up his studies. For the first time his mother came to Delhi when she was informed by his landlord that he was seriously ill. The poet didn't want anyone in his family to know about his hellish life in an unauthorized colony of Delhi. His mother used to get upset to see her son as a tenant and even she had lost her gold earrings and she wept for her loss in his absence. This incident proved to be a major turning point in poet's life. He left preparation for UPSC exams and minimized his expenses on social work so that he could have his own home through his savings. Finally with his hard work and dedication he could purchase his own home in Delhi within two years of this incident. He married Ms. Seema Anand with exceptional terms and conditions related to his social work so that she couldn't bind him down at home. She supports him whole heartedly to fulfill his dreams.

He gives full credit of his achievements to his family, especially to his mother for instilling in him values that are helping him to sail the life boat peacefully and successfully.

As a dedicated learner, academic success wasn't difficult for him, and he was a star student throughout his school and college days. He enrolled himself in the University of Delhi for a Bachelor's Degree, and later he did Elementary Teacher Education diploma from SCERT Delhi. He came in contact with gods in the form of ideal teachers throughout his journey. He feels gratitude to Late Dr. Bhagvati Prasad Dimri (Lecturer Hindi DIET Rajendra Nagar), Ms. Kanchan Roy (Asst. Professor Work Education and Vocational Education, DIET Moti Bagh), Dr. Lovely Puri (Asst. Professor, Life Skills, DIET Rajendra Nagar), and MS. Suman Bhatia (Reader SCERT, Delhi) whose ideals and principles encourage him time to time in his journey. He feels grateful to his ideal teacher Ms. Suman Bhatia for her regular motivation and support on many occasions. Words are not enough to express his gratitude towards his mentors. In reality teachers have helped him grow into the person he is and he is always thankful to his teachers for their help, support and guidance. After getting ETE diploma, he faced competition and got appointment as Asst. Teacher in MCD and did B.Ed from IGNOU along with his job. He got promotion as TGT but he was not satisfied with this post and prepared for the post of Lecturer of English in the Directorate of Education, Delhi and qualified. He loves teaching, and he never misses any opportunity to work as a social worker. To fulfill his dream of having ownership of the greatest academic center of the world, he prepared for UPSC exam for the post of Principal and now he is even shortlisted for interview. If he is finally selected for the same, then it would be the greatest opportunity for him to work for the poor people like him who are left behind only due to lack of opportunities. The poet requests all his readers to wish for his success so that he could materialize his sacred dreams.

In the year 2016 he got selection as a mentor teacher and became the part of government's educational reforms. From 2016 to 2021 he visited many educational institutions along with his fellow mentors and reputed educationists which opened his vision. He feels thankful to Directorate of Education, Delhi Government for introducing Mentorship programme and innovative practices in Delhi Government schools. He feels gratitude to Mentor of mentors, Mr.B.P.Pandey (OSD School Branch, DOE Delhi), Mr.Som Tyagi (Prabodhak & Educator Jeevan Vidya), Dr.Shyam Sunder Punia (Lecturer DIET Darya Ganj), Dr.Rajesh (Principal DIET Ghumanheda), Dr.Mukesh Aggarwal (Sr.Lecturer DIET Keshavpuram), Dr.Anil Teotia (Principal DIET Dilshad Garden & Chairman Happiness Curriculum), Ms.Mridula Aggarwal (Asst. Professor DIET Pitampura), Dr. Charu Varma (Asst. Professor DIET Pitampura) and all those who came in his contact and influenced his thoughts in anyway.

As a mentor teacher he mentored thousands of Delhi Government school teachers and facilitated education of lakhs of students in Delhi government schools. He got appreciation from all around. He got Excellence in Education Chunauti Awards 2017 for his remarkable job in the field of education.

As per the initiatives of the Directorate of Education he completed many Professional Development courses for his own capacity building-

Some important ones are as follows:

Teaching and Mentoring Leadership Programme from NIE, Singapore.

Learner Centered Classrooms from Regional English Language Office, U.S. Embassy, New Delhi.

The American English (AE) E-Teacher Program from Arizona State University, Sponsored by U.S. Dept of State, Funded By U.S. Government.

Beyond Mentoring: Imagining a Teacher Training MOOC from Regional English Language Office, Embassy of the United States of America, New Delhi.

And many more....

Along with his job, he completed master's degree in English, in Education and then in Social Work and Counseling from IGNOU, Delhi. He received many appreciation letters from reputed organizations for his extra ordinary work in the field of education. In addition, he serves as a social reformer for Aaryawart Charitable and Welfare Society. He is a founder member of this NGO, and spends considerable time and resources for the betterment of common people. Even during the Covid pandemic he did not stay indoors like others. He distributed food on daily basis and was honored with Corona Warrior certificates from many organizations.

This book took eleven years to complete. He received so much encouragement and positive feedback from his friends and students that he couldn't stop writing.

He feels gratitude towards his family members, friends, relatives, and those who assisted him in any way to complete this book. He feels thankful to Blue Rose Publication and Team for their full support. He extends special appreciation and gratitude for his colleague Ms. Kiran for her great support in completing this project.

He is hoping that his first publication, "Mango Man" will enjoy grand success.

"Where do I run off from fixed God's grand goal?
Does omnipresent God reside only at shrines?
Someone needs my body, someone hires my soul,
But neither my body is free nor my soul confines."

About The Book

"Mango Man" is the song of commons,
Story of insight indicates never fraud.
Common man's journey is usually blocked by demons,
But each and every step for good is assisted by God.

"Mango man" is not only a poem but also an echo of heart of common people. Emotions of this poem are colored with different devices, idioms, phrases and quotes. "Life Turns and Turns Around" is one of the best examples of motivational poems. Mango Man portrays the plight of common people whereas **Mangoism** desires such type of ism where a common man gets equal opportunity to grow. The third part of Mango Man is "Mango Mind" which is centered on the worldly wise ways to grow and flourish. **"Quick Fox, Lazy Dog"** covers all the sounds of language like all the colors of life whereas next poem, **"Quicker Quacks, Lazy Lacks"** covers each alphabet of the poem **"Quick Fox, Lazy Dog"** and a **very lengthy poem of Acrostic style in English Literature**. The poet has employed many poetic devices in the poem and plays with words so beautifully that a literature lover can find all essential tools that a poet uses to create rhythm, enhance poem's meaning, intensify mood and feelings of a common man. "Quicker

Quacks, Lazy Lacks" also illustrates one root word in different forms and it is a **most beautiful poem of Acrostic style ever written in English Literature**. Similar to Anadiplosis and Anaphora,Epistrophe is used to emphasize emotions and to give rhythm and wings to mango man. **"Love Leads Life"** is the best example of literary skill, Symploce". This poem is a satire on our society and so many stanzas of this poem keep many meanings. The last poem, **"Litigation"** is a satire on our rich friendly system and the same was presented to Honorable Chief Justice of Supreme Court in year 2014 as a part of Public Interest Litigation. **Each part of "Mango Man" is the superb example of literary piece ever covered in English Literature.**

Idea of this poem came to the poet's mind during the Indian anti-corruption movement, popularly known as Anna Andolan, which was a series of demonstrations and protests across India that began in 2011 and was intended to establish strong legislation and enforcement against perceived endemic political corruption. The movement aimed to alleviate corruption from the Indian government with the introduction of the Jan Lokpal Bill. The movement was primarily one of non-violent civil resistance and was composed of demonstrations, marches, acts of civil disobedience, hunger strikes, and rallies, and the use of social media to organize, communicate, and raise awareness. Forms of corruption may vary, but can include bribery, lobbying, extortion, cronyism, nepotism, parochialism, patronage, influence peddling, graft, and embezzlement. Misuse of government power for other purposes, such as repression of political opponents and general police brutality, is also considered as political corruption. The activities that constitute illegal corruption differ depending on the country or jurisdiction. For instance, some political funding practices that are legal in one place may be illegal in another. Worldwide bribery alone is estimated to involve over 1 trillion US dollars annually. A state of unrestrained political corruption is **known as a Kleptocracy**, literally meaning **"Rule By Thieves"**. During these movements the poet passed through sleepless nights to solve these burning issues but felt helpless. He started to show his anger on papers and started to write "Mango Man" . The poet has taken more than 10 years to cover all colors of social, economical as well as political life. The poet has tried to introduce "Mango Man" through its first part **"Mango Face"** and the other parts of this poem are attempts to portray complete picture of a common man. Cover page of this book says millions of words and designed by the poet himself with the help of his students. He feels gratitude to all his students who have assisted him to color his imagination into beautiful picture. He feels special thanks to Ms. Prachi, Ms. Suhasini, Mr. Rehan and

Ms. Tanya for their full heartedly cooperation and support to design this book.

Readers are expected to go through this poem for deep introspection and poet is willing to have their valuable suggestions at _whistleblowersatishanand@gmail.com_ for further improvement. "Mango Man" is first publication of the poet so he is very hopeful for full support and motivation.

"Mango Man" is not the song of a single man,
"Mango Man" is not the lesson for a single man.
"Mango Man" is not the satire on a single man,
So, with high spirit, get ready to meet Mango Man.

Table of Contents

MANGO MAN

1. "Mango Face" (Introduction)

Maa Saraswati ideates her fan,
Maa Luxmi provides resources,
All gods bless blissfully mango man,
Maa Durga strengthens and forces.

"Mango Man" is the song of commons,
Story of insight indicates never fraud.
Common man's journey is usually blocked by demons,
But each and every step for good is assisted by God.

Literature leads life to live peacefully,
Literary devices and tools are to beautify insight.
When emotional flows are twined together mindfully,
Each section of "Mango Man" seems sun like bright.

"Mango Man" is a satire on society,
"Mango Mind" is the most motivational.
Its each and every word affirm universality,
Showing sounds of rational irrational.

Emotions flow with," Life Turns And Turns Around",
"Quick Fox, Lazy Dog" covers sounds like all colors of life.
"Quicker Quacks, Lazy Lacks" reflects commons' sound,
Love is a natural instinct for all lives as, "Love Leads Life."

Only God knows what is in store for "Mango Man" ,
"Love leads life", and learnt life eagerly learns lesson.
Literary devices are to emphasize importance of man,
Loop holes of our system are covered in, "Litigation".

Anaphora and Epistrophe create sweet rhythm,
Acrostic style of literary device makes readers fan.
Even echo of heart creates natural logarithm,
Symploce, and Anadiplosis, are used to beautify man.

Some parts present common man's challenges,
Another part feeds motivation to introspect.
Words are decorated with idioms and phrases,
All poetic devices and quotes links linguistic aspect.

Life like poem is adorned with different devices,
Struggle like story of failure is more fertile.
Tussle continues between virtues and vices,
Poetic devices move mango man to relax for a while.

Childhood is golden, adulthood is twisted,
"Mango Man" starts journey with simplicity.
Proceeds, knowing that struggles are already listed,
And with miracles of God's grace gets maturity.

Childhood passes in search of joy,
And adulthood passes in search of pod.
Golden bird booed, but becomes time's toy,
Spirits surrender searching salvation under the feet of
God.

"Mango Man" is not the song of a single man,
"Mango Man" is not the lesson for a single man.
"Mango Man" is not the satire on a single man,
So, with heavy heart, get ready to peep into Mango Man.

BY: -   SATISH ANAND

2. Life Turns And Turns Around

Life turns and turns around,
There is more noise little bit sound;
Echo of heart is left unheard,
Lion is harassed hearing herd.

Precious time moves very fast,
Rest is rust, reduces one's cost;
Be updated, march with the time;
Who is interested in listening old rime?

Temporary scars recover someday,
New leaves come out in the May;
Without autumn no spring shines,
Neither God resides in only shrines.

Accept challenges, face devils on the way,
Easy opportunity rarely knocks all the day;
Mainly money minded, buttering buddy tries to bar,
Still, success stories succeed from scar.

Don't expect from others to win for you,
Tiger never likes to hunt in the zoo;
Finally, fate favours the brave in the war,
Be permanent star, says the twinkling star.

BY: - SATISH ANAND

3. Mango Man

I am sole overburdened mango man of trampled soul,
My national house is mortgaged by multinational laps.
Body parts are trafficked, transplanted to slay sole soul,
Ideology of protean opportunist cap can anytime lapse.

Supreme shark soars in sovereign shallow sandy seas
Pillars of power play puppet show just beating the air.
Prince puts heart and soul but freedom is sure to seize,
Democracy disappears into thin air for autocratic heir.

"Mango Man" is not the song of a single man,
"Mango Man" is not the lesson for a single man.
"Mango Man" is not the satire on a single man,
So, with heavy heart, get ready to peep into Mango Man.

I am a mango man,
I am always cheated.
No one is my fan,
I am always ill treated.

    I am very simple,
    I am always insulted.
    My face wears a dented dimple,
    Is without love, life resulted?

No one respects me,
I am very dejected.
Is bee hive possible without bee?
Why roots are always ejected?

> I am a drum like hound,
> I am always beaten.
> I cry for better sound,
> Otherwise I am threaten.

What do I deserve,
Disgust, disgrace, or disdain?
Why do my rights reserve,
To get glory, grace or gain?

> I am a grounded mango tree,
> Hardly have I survived for long.
> In the storms millions of flowers set free,
> Fear stricken my offspring never sings spring song.

I am very colorful,
But there is no color in my life.
Everyone's behavior is scornful,
My neck is always under knife.

> I am extremely ensured,
> I am to be surely replaced.
> As if my heart is life time insured,
> Granted freely whenever it's claimed.

I am trodden,
I have no right.
My name is forgotten,
Now it's an identity's fight.

    I am a mango man,
    I am always hanged.
    I tour on mercy van,
    My soul is always banged.

I am a think tank,
My brain is used for others.
I never get thank,
I am thrown into gutters.

    I am very bright,
    My intelligence is for corporates.
    I never get my right,
    Different markets have my different rates.

I am not convent educated,
I am not civilized.
My behavior is not fabricated,
So my dreams are never materialized.

    I am forced for vocational training,
    As if my body is designed for skill learning.
    They get professional training,
    And my skill is used for their earning.

I am ill fed,
My mind is full of desires.
Bread and butter is at others shed,
My heart is always on fires.

> I am of mango man's breeds,
> My God resides at barren land.
> I perspire for spoilt seeds,
> Does lotus bloom on dry sand?

My land is purely infertile,
I grow like stubborn weed.
High yielded seeds are only for fertile,
I need neither fertilizer nor seed.

Society is meant for few fugitives fertile,
Millionaires move with political weedicides.
Millions weeds hosting few millionaires as pest is futile,
Whereas pests deserve to be treated by pesticides.

> Educated unaware guides my senses,
> Uneducated aware is my guide.
> My poor education decides preferences,
> My bright career is having its black side.

Neither my mind nor my soul is customized,
I am a sole proprietor of a sunken soul.
Auction is fixed, and rate is finalized,
Either of my body or of my soul.

Where do I run off from God's goal?
Does omnipresent God reside at only shrines?
Someone needs my body, someone hires my soul,
But neither my body is free nor my soul confines.

I can concentrate on my studies,
But my concentration power is seized.
I am a free slave of unrealistic hobbies,
Otherwise my top-bottom is bridged.

My close relatives are open teachers,
Unskilled drivers drive my rusted motor.
I am fed up with platonic preachers,
Skilled trained teachers never sense sensor.

I am on such a way,
There is nothing to eat, nothing to drink.
Politicians even digested the hay,
We are left thirsty, standing on the brink.

My little cottage is my hub,
No other palace has its link.
They bathe in pond or tub,
We have little water to sink.

My efforts to rise make me sick,
Overtime work is everlasting.
I burn like a candle without wick,
I can survive on regular fasting.

I am very hard working,
I perspire full day vigorously.
Laborers are slaves, not king,
My fuel is only to burn continuously.

In a cloudy mind millions of stars peep,
Soul seeks stars but body is bunkered.
A little liquor leads sound sleep,
People call me a daredevil drunkard.

I am to be defamed only,
No one tries to understand my situation.
This world is ours, but feels lonely,
Train is to halt at every station.

At every station, people gather like herd,
Masters talk having their own tower.
Without signal, I just ponder my world,
Only circumstances grant me some power.

My power is overpowered,
I live on others neath.
Braves never care coward,
A healthy mind has an easy breath.

I am habitual of starvation,
Even unable to digest water.
What for bread, without digestion,
It is an exchange like boner barter.

I am the worst needy,
My needs never end.
My friends always greedy,
In problems, refusal is their trend.

I am inherited such a beautiful personality,
I am rejected at first sight in every interview.
Innocent infant IQ is mine without duality,
But I am unaware about officers' view.

My sons are born without feather,
Only golden wings can soar or fly.
Mine wounded wings wander hither and thither,
They are destined to measure sky.

I am a by birth borrower,
Live on lenders liege.
My path is fixed narrower,
Otherwise my reputations seize.

Vicious victory poisons my ear,
I am disabled, defeated and defamed.
Others make fun, I always hear,
Being poor, I am only blamed.

I am not proud of my power,
My obligations usually eat my confidence.
Water fall looks better than shower,
Distant forest looks very dense.

Goddess promises for boon,
She asks me for my only desire.
Beautiful hut is needed under moon,
Some twigs for bread and free fire.

I dreamt for peaceful life,
Bread and butter to survive.
Little respect without strife,
There is neither honey nor hive.

In progress race we are banned,
Satan is adjudged as referee.
Our stamina is such a short spanned,
Victory is impossible, defeat is free.

I always face trouble,
Is it only to fuss?
Why am I to crumble,
For good governance or chaos?

People make fun of me,
As adversity is the greatest curse.
I am neither He nor She,
Incurable diseases have infinite course.

I am a homeless wanderer,
I live like a monk.
Journey passes like ponderer,
Dogs bark at beggars and people honk.

My struggle is to survive only,
Life drives, having driving ban.
Zoological garden frees beast lonely,
Is bonded beast better than man?

There is no inequality in the nature of God,
But gender differences are often pressed.
People remember same God by different lord,
Religious differences are often expressed.

No self respect, no self esteem,
Solid selfless Satan makes me confuse.
Why my light is always dim,
Is it breakdown of only fuse?

Right to information is on papers,
Is it for vote or hope?
Is it Kid in diapers?
Or is it only failure of dope?

We are mango people,
We are never heard.
They laugh at us and giggle,
We make sound only in herd.

Is it not unsolved riddle?
Where mist is never cleared?
No sound of music in my fiddle,
Color of rainbow only sometimes cheered.

I am an old fashioned computer,
My software is out dated.
My hardwares always clatter,
Virus in brain has deeply seated.

Insecure future, my personality ceases,
Inferiority complex always in my mind.
I have inherited incurable diseases,
Such a virus no one can find.

I am born without feather,
They are born with silver spoon.
I search sauce hither and thither,
They curse me with infinite boon.

I am just a number,
I am not a human.
Everyone uses my power,
I always remain common.

I am only a vote bank,
Shallow bank attracts for deep.
Selfish society makes me crank,
I am very weak and cheap.

Everyone wants to encash my honey,
No one comes to fulfill my need.
They are experts in making money,
Never feel guilty for their heinous deed.

He that hoards money,
Takes pain for others.
Riches have wings for journey,
Uneasy lies the head that crown wears.

I always vote for better future,
My right is used for others.
Our representatives harass and torture,
We have converted thieves into robbers.

I am always meekly murdered,
I play hide and seek with death.
Body is bound, and spirit strangled,
Life like lures lures and gasps for breath.

Death is destined at last for extra fasting,
Postmortem report also tells lie.
It's announced as organ trafficking,
Grieved heart has tensed mind and deep sigh.

I am panic stricken,
My mind cannot think properly.
Is massacre only meant to waken,
Or is it to relieve soul, murdered brotherly?

Workers are needed to work properly,
But why do they need mercy seekers?
Butchers need afraid beast bodily,
Who is an accomplice to massacres?

My life is never noticed,
But massacre is fully dramatized.
Media is advancely fixed,
Profit and share already sized.

When humanity is murdered,
Integrity gets suicide.
Soft music is being murmured,
Discussion over homicide or genocide.

Someone is hired as analyst,
Political butchers are welcomed from both sides.
Thousands of demonstrators congregate for feast,
After hunting mango men, everyone rides.

This time we are mute viewers,
We are united figurants.
Producers create rumours,
Our fleshes are sold to many merchants.

Someone says it murder,
Someone proclaims suicide.
Politicians think over,
But truth is always hide.

Poor public plays as beast,
They are always manly posed.
Leaders gather on funeral's feast,
Beautiful script with lyrics is composed.

Lifeless life lives lifelong,
Sinner survives long to pay penance.
Whom the God loves dies young,
Mango man has not any one hindrance.

Unsocial society says animated caricature,
Lifeless life leads lifelessness in life.
Mango man is a single celled social creature,
Multicellular devils dance with open knife.

I am a part of crowd,
No one recognizes me.
My caricature bears borrowed shroud,
Even my face disguises me.

My soul fights for justice,
But lawyers demand bribe.
System forces such fees,
As if I belong to a foreign tribe.

Litigation offers relief in public interest,
Mean motives stare poverty to expose.
Judiciary hosts millions of pest,
Scant sources sink case to dispose.

Honorable judge asked for witnesses,
Witnesses can be bought or sold.
Truth is rusted without oil faces,
Lead is polished like genuine gold.

Judges need golden papers on board,
Reputed lawyers are to put point.
Justice is free but process is gold,
Long lasting journey only to disappoint.

I lose hope for my own rights,
Story of failure is always closed.
My sons blame me too for my fights,
Struggle for justice is never disclosed.

Beautiful message for all preachers,
Live like slave without making noise.
System is good, but meant for richers,
Poor pleads to gods of devils in disguise.

Justice is denied in absence of papers,
Papers are made of golden size.
Money matters more for genuine prayers,
Loser's symbol is rewarded as a prize.

Opposition makes fun and family blames,
My integrity is always exposed.
Everyone announces fraud and shames,
In absence of honest witnesses, case is disposed.

I get punishment of doubt,
I am always chained and jailed.
Judges give them grant of doubt,
They get parole or bailed.

I die in hope of judgment,
My innocence never proved.
They die without judgment,
Their real faces are never broomed.

It is a matter of personal interest,
Free of cost justice, no one can.
Justice adds costs commutative interest,
Is it cremation or burial of a man?

Cremation or burial is common man's death,
Soul wanders until rest.
Lenders search till last breath,
Whereas relatives get busy in guzzling feast.

My plea is always overruled and unheard,
Why am I forced to say, my Lord?
We are seen as uncivilized beard,
I die early in hope of Honorable God.

Unblessed, unlucky, unhappy, unaided,
Startled, standing empty handed.
Flower unbloomed until faded,
Leaving segregated suppressed strangled stranded.

I am a ferocious dog,
I bark at relative's beggars.
Everyone having their own log,
Owns smile hides devil's draggers.

Who is my own?
What is mine?
Sorrow seeds are sown,
Nothing seems fine.

I am a day dreamer,
My dream is for no one's meant.
I am like an inexperienced swimmer,
Who usually returns empty hands, face faint?

I'm a mellow mango,
I can fall any time.
In disturbed mid sea, in overloaded cargo,
I am roaring in detuned rime.

My caliber is always examined,
My ability is always checked.
I am always fined,
I am never backed.

It's my pen,
That feels very tired.
Body is in pain,
Soul seems retired.

My seed is sown,
But my crop is already hired.
Mind is my own,
But my heart is fired.

My poverty adds fuel to the fire,
Relatives add insult to injury.
The world seems dark and dire,
Bloody tears rains like fury.

I am torn in my family,
Everyone's demands are unique.
No one is happy with me,
Their confrontation causes critique.

I am not so resourceful,
How can I manage them all?
My sound is always regretful,
How much one can fall?

It is deprived, depressed and distressed I,
Puppy gets respected more than me.
He is civilized and shy,
I am an unwanted brute butter bee.

I can never get my promised land,
I can't earn easy money.
My jaundiced eye breaks the job in hand,
Why do I desire for pure honey?

Beauty is not only skin deep,
Beauty lies in the eye of the beholder.
My poor heart tries to peep,
Beautiful eyes, kind heart and shoulder.

My reputation is always at stake,
Arrogant society can crush it any time.
My identity is usually called fake,
It costs not a single dime.

I am a dilettante devotee,
I am a sensible superstitious.
My wisdom is at sea,
My logic is always suspicious.

Wisdom is better than strength,
Knowledge is power inside.
Silence holds enemy at arm's length,
Learning like Lords, leads long ride.

My mother makes me my mentor,
Father forces for foul fruited.
Sour smiles show showy sensor,
Unaided unidentified units unable usually unsuited.

Whenever my dearer loves,
Their extreme love makes me blind.
Mother, father, sisters or brothers,
Their selfish motive seems behind.

Our bond is so strong,
No one can cut even shadow.
The world tries to prove us wrong,
But in different bodies, same blood flow.

Scarcity is the root of all evils,
Wounds of dear ones never hide.
Beggars are born without wills,
Dreams are hired just for a ride.

What is the use of the constitution,
If everyone needs only two times bread?
Very few hoards rampant ration,
Does poorer live without head?

My body is designed for bearance,
Their body is meant for comfort.
Why nature has created this difference,
Do flowers ever bloom in the dirt?

Life is not, what others see,
It wears not a single face.
Deep hills are hidden inside deep sea,
But it stages smooth sea surface.

Life likes love like liver,
Death dreads dear darling's desires desirely.
Blood flows like purified river,
Endless end ends end entirely.

Life is full of dangers,
Death is full of joy.
Danger damages my deed daggers,
Life and death is each other's toy.

I am destiny's puppet,
Devil decides derailed destiny.
Brutes blow their own trumpet,
As if Mango Man is very tiny.

I am a poor devotee,
I expense, what I save.
My God never gets happy,
Nothing is left, what I have.

I am a justified judge,
Judge of my own crimes.
Reward or punishment, I held a grudge,
Blaming others always in my own rhymes.

I am a malleable mango,
Mango of ordinary class.
Firm farmers need to grow,
Brittle ones break like glass.

Here hides hapless hero helplessly,
Helpless header hoards hidden heat.
Truant termagant throws thump termagantly,
Twitter tweets tactless tweet.

System in my left, system in my right,
I am to march for March.
Scattered system stimulates partial plight,
I just wait for roofless rootless starch.

Either my ladder is always short,
Or my top is a little bit high.
My hut always looks like a fort,
But not a single pigeon can fly.

I am a soft target for all,
My belongings are safe unsafe.
I am a standing joke to call,
Neither my property nor my name is safe.

My all energy is to drain,
Jaundiced eye can never see.
Heart is not ready to listen brain,
It's a conflict between I and me.

I am a mango man,
I am always cheated.
No one is my fan,
I am always mistreated.

I am burdened with poor forefathers,
My ethics make me sick.
Responsibilities of loans my father gathers,
As our blood is very thick.

I live from hand to mouth,
Why do my half hearted efforts never fit?
Magnet signals only North and South,
For hard working people, sky is the limit.

I am over head and ears in debt,
I born in it, live in it, and I would die.
Why my forefathers and sons having same fate?
When would time change, when would destiny shy?

I want to start my business,
No one allows giving me loan.
System guarantees only for riches,
But I have nothing to pawn.

I am fair and square in all my dealings,
My upbringing and values are suspected.
Question mark over my dignity hurts feelings,
Vicious circle trap makes my heart infected.

Why do people afraid of me?
I have neither horn nor poisonous teeth.
Society has neither face nor clarity,
What does it show and what does it hide beneath?

No one opt the judge, who fails in his own family,
That's why; I don't poke my nose in others affairs.
But people pass comments and raise questions silly,
Why have their times to intervene in my matters?

I face odds on daily basis,
Nature gives lesson time to time.
I can bear toughest crisis,
Learning to defense is never a crime.

I am like a fish out of water,
My gills are damaged due to over burden.
When I need lungs, why can I not barter?
Is it also mismanagement of natural warden?

A snake in the grass attacks over me silently,
I only try to defense myself.
When power is not enough to kill an enemy completely,
One needs only to secure oneself.

I feel joy occasionally,
I try to find it in small things.
Why do I never prepare mentally?
Can I not hear music, if someone sings?

Pen is mightier than missiles,
The more one learn, the more one earn.
I know, I am to march miles and miles,
But when opportunity knocks, why am I unable to discern?

There is no limit of learning,
The more I learn, the more I yearn.
But there must be a limit for earning,
The more you earn, the less you burn.

I plod like tortoise,
Rich rabbit runs very fast.
My loads make much noise,
I get confused and turn at last.

Everyone promises to love me, love my dog,
But I always lose my heart.
I am neutral blind lovers' log,
Which is used in selfish cart.

I am not a mad dog,
A dog's life is better than I.
You may call me a rainy frog,
Who lives neither on land nor on sky.

My path is full of thorns and scars,
It's a long road that knows no turning.
My target goes farse and farse,
When I make full efforts to do something.

Slaves are born bond free,
But always take rest in chains.
How one can see tiny tall tree,
When eyes are wet with dry rains.

I am not an awardee,
Neither I get rewarded.
My motivation makes me hardy,
But my fuel never gets regarded.

When I fly for a break,
Caged bird loses command over wings.
They call me a featherless freak,
Because bondage only wails, never sings.

My language is known unknown,
Under stand I am unable to understand.
Whistle of revolution is only blown,
Major mishappenings happen under big hand.

Unable to understand my own voice,
Some says soft stubborn stupid stranger.
I accept, who asks for loser's choice?
Determined dangerous daredevil distrains danger.

Sound of heart is known unknown,
Biased unbiased echo is heard unheard.
Soft stubborn seeds stay sown unsown,
Broken pieces are broken by banning bird.

I am just like a hollow coconut,
My tears make homes inside bark bars.
Doors of open heart and brain remain shut,
Just as a sweet smile hides deepest scars.

I lose my battle again and again,
But always fight to be a Juggler.
I am unaware about my train,
My shadow tries to cheat as burglar.

I am a genuine green horn,
Identified ideal inexperienced Indian is I.
Have you ever seen a rose without thorn,
As only few stars shine in the cloudy sky?

The deeper one falls, the higher one rises,
The higher one rises, the harder one falls.
Without the sun set not a single sun rises,
Best comes out of most difficult goals.

When in Rome do as the Romans do,
I live in my dream world lonely.
Blind followers are just friendly foe,
My fight is with the Pope only.

A friendly foe is more dangerous,
Than an unfriendly open foe.
Neither friend among foes moulds rigorous,
Nor united enemies ever stand in a row.

My pocket is too small,
To adjust my friends inside.
Devil dodgers are too tall,
To hide in a cell inside.

My destiny is caged in a cell,
My all roads lead to Rome.
I wander in my tiny cell,
Virtual house is declared my home.

Everyone preaches me to limit my sky,
To cut my coat according to my cloth.
My tiny tower can never be high,
As body realizes reality, but soul refuses oath.

I pose myself as generous in society,
I burn candle at both ends.
Whenever I invest in society for royalty,
Life takes U turn and bends.

Money makes the mare go,
Necessity has no particular law.
Poverty strikes in full flow,
Needy ones make man of straw.

I am an old fashioned machine,
My motor is always seized.
Updated version is in the scheme,
Till then I am being greased.

I am a born politician brand,
My politics begins at womb.
Each one having their own demand,
Unlimited limits bar me till dome.

My foetus passes through radiation,
Mother examines again and again.
Survival seems sweet poison,
It is like labored easy pain.

Borrowing adds as births-rebirths legacy,
Interest, penalties, even late charges are charged.
Principal stands like despotic democracy,
Tragic end meets with Comic relief merged.

I am a peter pan,
Maturity never comes to me.
I stumble over again and again,
Free suggestions I get without fee.

I work like a Trojan,
But Trojan horse opposes my rise.
My strengths are hired by opposition,
I am engulfed by world's worldly wise.

Failure-success seems side by side,
Destiny stares the state of the face.
Reality seems poles apart to ride,
Usually I fail in my own race.

Now and again my heart is dressed,
It is meant either to be tamed or toyed.
Crushed, chopped, chafed, compressed,
Identity has been declared null and void.

I am as fit as fiddle entirely,
My vision is as clear as day.
My potential is to spread like fiery,
Cruel circumstances call it a day.

All men are created equal eaters,
Equality exists on papers only.
All is not gold that glitters,
Smiling faces wear faces lonely.

My love is genuine, but beloved is far,
Everybody is ready to declare her jilt.
Heart is wounded having unseen scar,
Mind is full of unforeseen guilt.

Nearby faces can't be seen properly,
Distant people seem closer to us.
When you wake up its morning's early,
Even our own face disguises us.

Eligibility for heaven is kingly end,
Nothing is wrong with beautiful hell.
New ways open only when old ones bend,
After all, All's well that ends well.

Anti abets "All is fair in love and war",
Inequality exists like Bay of Bengal.
Love with whom or whom with war,
Poor pale face is wrapped with torn pall.

I am all in all of my family,
I try my best to justify all squares.
Expectations are high of all and sundry,
Each one is ready to be trapped in snares.

All of a sudden lifeless life gets spoil,
Bull struggles to manage all the time.
Nothing seems suitable, but bulls moil,
Blessed beast's life costs a single dime.

Hand hires homeless homely herds,
I easily lose my temper and heart.
My blind eyes says a million words,
But people peep inside me to hurt.

I am an illegitimate child of my country,
I have been treated step motherly since birth.
My only national father clings only to monetary,
I have become habitual to survive in the dearth.

My emotions and feelings are cheapest in the world,
No one cares about my heart, body and soul.
My body is used badly; my heavy heart is hurled,
No one comes to me without prefixed goal.

My beloved is a top class infidel,
Air is easily available to everyone all time.
My brain is polluted; heart is on fire, soul rebel,
I can only regret over my precious spent time.

I am the stuff of squeezed sugarcane,
I am left with no taste anymore.
To give others sweetness, I take only pain,
My earth is hollow without any core.

My brain is not so developed,
I am unable to find logic behind.
My body is always ready to be eloped,
Knowing that, this cruel world would never be kind.

This world is made only to deceive me,
Everyone comes for their own benefits.
No one really truly loves for me,
In selfish cart poor adjustable wheels easily fits.

I am a little sparrow,
My nest is very small at corner.
My freedom is very narrow,
In my own land I live like a foreigner.

People stare at me, as if I am not a human,
Everybody wants to trample me as their foot path.
I have been rejected since childhood, what I can,
If I am a sinner, do I not need holy bath?

Darkness of sin is increasing day by day,
Puppets only watch games, never plays.
O God! Why are sinners flourishing rather than pay?
O God! Where are you busy these days?

O Mango Man! When would you realize your
strength?
O Mango man! Why do you not refuse to be a
puppet?
O Mango Man! Why do you leave success at arm's
length?
O God! How can one play anyone's trumpet?

My heart is as soft as broken pieces of icebergs,
It melts very easily to see heat around.
In my womb I swallow ancient burgs,
It groans on hearing wandering souls' sound.

> As long as life can confine,
> As long as inequality can exist,
> As long as sun soars to uniformly shine,
> God exists everywhere to partially assist.

My spirit ends like black hole,
My lenders continuously revolve around.
Attackers deviate at poles without goal,
Even no one can see my dark ground.

> My tears are nothing, but my pleasure,
> My struggle is nothing, but my exercise.
> Even my measurable pain no one can measure,
> As my disappeared appearances always guise.

My day is my night; my night is my day,
My cool mind keeps me always hot.
My autumn is May, my spring is May,
My no states yes, my yes hides not.

> I am a migrant labourer,
> My sigh of pain seems harsh Horner.
> For my family, I am sole enabler.
> In my own land I chirp like foreigner.

My path is full of thorns and tweet,
No one else can walk over it.
There are so many blisters in my feet,
No one else is ready to talk about it.

I am like a woodpecker,
I have to work hard for a little food.
My struggle to survive, no one can measure,
My life begins at woods and ends at wood.

 I fall under the influence very easily,
 My compulsions have made me very weak.
 I easily accept even a deal of loss daily,
 I bet burnt log by losing transcendent timber teak.

My life is passing in searching opportunity,
But not an opportunity is being found.
Seed is latent, unborn without maturity,
How can a plant grow without ground?

 I am a latent seed all the time,
 Dormancy dreams for fair dream world.
 Unfair state stops singing same old rhyme,
 Different hides hide hide in different world.

My future is painted as black as ink,
I struggle all the year around.
Reality is far, having no present link,
Heart and mind make different sound.

I am a flowering fern of spring,
But not a flower one can see.
Either the months of summer or spring,
Not a cooking leaf is there on a tree.

I am always obliged for compensations,
System is for starvation but famine makes me bold.
Failure after failure I taste in near succession,
So that body gets tremble with fear and blood gets cold.

I am a homeless wanderer,
I need shelter from rain.
I am known as blunderer,
My family beg only for mouthful grain.

I am purchased and sold to get loan settle,
Knowing that I'd never repay it tomorrow;
I know, my source of income would always be little,
But humiliated life seems better to die of starvation and sorrow.

I blame others knowing I am wrong,
I am also prepared to throw my excuses.
I am accustomed as well to sing same song,
Actually grieved heart and negative mindset always fuses.

Nature gives me little loss,
But unnatural elements try to maximize.
My God is my master, my God is my boss,
Political birds are here only to dramatize.

I am a mindless mango man,
My existence is badly hurt.
Own life has imposed on me life ban,
How can I forget stories of flirt?

This life is an extinguished light,
Nothing is here rather than regret.
How anyone can make water ignite,
It is grieved heart that quenches only to forget.

My body is an old fashioned cart,
That has been flying like a threadless kite.
Finally fugitive brain may forget heart,
But broken mirror can never unite.

Mango seed is manly sown,
Still sex shows his inequality.
Even if his religion is unknown,
But his caste hints his inability.

It's my poor pen,
It feels extremely tired.
Brain gets lighten in the rain,
But amidst dark clouds heart gets fired.

Daring dreams dare from dawn to dusk,
Spirit wanders aimlessly in dense wood.
Serpentine enemy hides inside deer musk,
Straight trees are usually cut for wood.

Hunter hunts hornbills here and there,
How can hornbills hide their beak?
Beautiful beak is as if Arabian nightmare,
Sometimes disguised blessings make one weak.

    My instincts blame my stars,
    My stars are always favourable.
    My destiny declares undeclared wars.
    Wars of any type are always unfavourable.

Poor struggles, fishes survive,
Soul sleeps at last.
Money misses, whales strike,
Destiny hits very fast.

    Poverty breeds curse,
    Goddess grants gold to gold.
    Fate favours only heavy purse,
    Terrorized poor's blood runs cold.

Tear gland originates unending ocean,
Shattered dreams, desert desires flow inside.
Himalayan ice melts fast, is wrong notion,
Ups and downs tides tear side by side.

    More they live, more they tense,
    More they live, more they perish.
    Tears tears all around to sense,
    Ocean flows but whales to cherish.

My obligations are known far and wide,
Each one comes to have its benefits.
Monstrous misfortune moves side by side,
I always wear the shoe that never fits.

      God resides in the have-nots' soul,
      The haves search it in the temples.
      The poor unchurches church by heavy soul,
      The riches bargains with gift samples.

I live in a fool's paradise,
Better to be a king of hell.
How can cell dwellers rise,
If ladder is just a mirage to dispel?

      Heavenly gifts are never biased,
      Cottage behind palace are always hide.
      Pure souls lose amongst devils disguised,
      Kings rehabilitates slaves side by side.

Flesh and blood of my family is very cheap,
Food security is the first and foremost duty.
Spirit's assassination wounds- incurable and deep,
Firstly I seek food and shelter for security.

      Failure knows every cloud has a silver lining,
      Clouds try to bring everything under the sun.
      Endless nights end with stars' shining,
      Lessons from failure make us run, run and run.

My each planning falls flat,
Need analysis seems me complex composite.
Echo of heart usually says this or that,
Objectives are still far from opposite.

     Justice is still a far cry,
     Sheep stands still in a long line.
     Court of tear glands has become dry,
     But a fish out of water looks fine.

Birds of same feather flock together,
Paid media's heroes are licensed pests.
Under an umbrella thick skinned beneficiaries gather,
And everyone tries to feather their own nests.

     Assured assurance assures assurances,
     Poverty peeps hope through desperate eyes.
     Back benchers get limited chances,
     No one is ready to listen their cries.

Love begets love, hatred begets hatred,
Oppressed oppressor oppresses oppressions oppressively.
Heartless enmity resides in the red,
Contempt is expected to contribute contempt massively.

     Jack is meant for deadly king,
     Jackless jack jacks jack.
     Even a tiger behaves friendly in the ring,
     But question is that," Is camel safe without back?"

I am an adopted orphan,
My God father lives in temples only.
Flickering candle looks like sun,
Lightening lights resemble hope closely.

> Nectar is trapped by honey bees,
> Crownless Kings are sent to royal jail.
> Success seeks sourced fees,
> Poisoned ear manages master fail.

God! O God! You hear me cry!
Millions of your sons sleep without food.
God! O God! You make tears dry!
Millions of your sons live in the wood.

> Boundless boundaries bind bond with God,
> Extreme hardships are sufficient to ignite.
> Beggars and idols are like two peas in a pod,
> Usually unsure surety ensures sure sureties to unite.

When I get ill,
Only lenders pray for my life.
When life loses its will,
Even parasites shoot to sharp knife.

> Usually I tell a lie,
> My truth never sounds solid.
> Souls seals inside and die,
> Inner feelings are crushed under the lid.

There is a tussle between body and soul,
Body demands comforts time to time.
Soul is the sole heir of bottomless sole,
Both sing traditionals of their old time.

    I am a manageable modest maid,
    Dominance of sex shuns married maiden.
    Foreign outlook courts homely made,
    As pure gold is veiled inside base leaden.

Real India lives in the villages,
Materialistic outlook runs towards towns.
Rural life has its own advantages,
Nothing is homely under silky gowns.

    Riches are unmarried bachelors,
    Their limit is unlimited sky.
    Materialistic world never values lovers,
    Lifeless lives naturally die.

Only tired traveller rests beside maiden road,
Red signal still warns danger before.
Pure gold is not made of leaden hoard,
It all depends on mine's reserves of ore.

    Poverty never spares time for beauty,
    Maiden's obligations make her mild.
    Red signal hides diamond under veils of duty,
    As a diamond in the hands of a child.

The world is never favorable to a poor,
A pretty peach waits when he works like donkey.
Relatives make fun, family calls him boor,
People comments, "grapes in the hands of a monkey."

    Freedom is fair, fat and forty,
    Though it seems beautiful.
    Since slavery shapes the minds shorty,
    These thoughts trims thoroughly thoughtless
    thoughts dutiful.

I am a bonded teacher,
My contractor doesn't know ABCD.
Poor performer produces poor preacher,
But bulls of a man seems ever ready.

    I am an amended mentor,
    I work under King's crown.
    Democratic mentees are self creator,
    Poor administration adds ups and down.

I don't deserve any award,
As award needs luxurious lubrication.
Milk is kept under cat as a guard,
But my station is far from destination.

    I am never being noticed,
    I am always ignored.
    My sufferings and pains are unnoticed,
    Even my stories make others bored.

I teach others a lesson,
A lesson of my own class.
I am known as nation's mason,
But only meant for bricks, stones and grass.

 Teaching is like learning lesson,
 Learning is like little maturity.
 Maturity makes updated modern mason,
 Mason usually gets ground zero with gratuity.

I am a careless scholar,
My books seem boring burden.
I am both ruled and ruler,
So body and brain bow down with overburden.

 I neither care for my studies,
 Nor I pay attention to teachers.
 I opt present, keeping future on lease,
 Well-wishers seem to me poor preachers.

I am an early bird for masters,
I wander hither and thither for their bread.
My bread and butter is disasters,
So my existence is always in the red.

 I eat like a bird,
 Even my senses never satisfy.
 My habitat is hired herd,
 So my wishes are only meant to justify.

My pearls of wisdom are hilarious for all,
I usually live in the seventh heaven.
I am fed up with my rise and fall,
In my mind, only kingly dreams are woven.

    I have been struggling to live like a king,
    But my path passes through a gang of beggars.
    Princess would propose me with diamond ring,
    But inheritance opposes to speak daggers.

Why are my kids not sent to mars?
At least they won't see others toys.
Even my sons survive facing billions bars,
Their real exploiter hides behind who employs.

    I am a modest mango man,
    I try my best to satisfy all till last breath.
    Everyone exploits extremely as much as one can,
    Finally people don't miss making pickles after my death.

My body as well as soul is too much selfish,
Even death doesn't fail to bargain or deal.
With such a confidence I take everyone's promise,
As if whosoever pays tribute tends to heal.

    People spare love for my death,
    They cry bitterly when I pass.
    Repentance remains reserve till last breath,
    Near ones seems showy, nothing more than mango
    mass.

The farther from the heart, louder it cries,
There is no limit of the duplicity of the people.
Neither sound seems sour nor tears allies,
Fabricated behavior is the modern way to wheedle.

> The world makes different rules for itself,
> The world makes different rules for others.
> Everyone desires heaven for himself,
> But why do they desire hell for others?

Society seeks sons sweet sober,
But behaves rudely to mothers.
People expect from those who are closer,
Why do we forget that we get what we give to others?

> My own life looks priceless but others life has no value,
> I want to seize every chance of life or breath.
> I want to win the race alone by saying others statue,
> Even my selfishness never hesitates to dodge dear
> death.

My journey begins with the soil,
I keep myself immature for long time.
My journey plods with my tough toil,
I rarely get reward for my hard time.

> My journey ends in the same soil,
> But it tastes something bitter.
> Why does my journey begin only to moil?
> Why not my genuine golden gold gleams glitter?

No matter who is at fault?
I am the one to be proved only culprit,
Punishment is already fixed and at halt,
But my soul is yet to be split.

> I am a mute spectator,
> I don't have right to make any comment.
> I am still dirty water,
> I am also a cleaning agent.

Just on this pretext, I get a little employment kind,
I don't have time to think more than myself.
What do I have to do with cleaning the river or mind?
I don't have sources to give more than myself.

> Jobless growth is going on, but country is shining,
> I am happy development is happening in my name.
> Even linkage exists between growth and nature's
> mining,
> But undoubtedly welfare is going on not only for the fame.

My festivals are only to make me realise of my scarce sources,
How can I match with highly resourced others?
On the one hand I depend on full moon without torches,
On the other hand neither my sons happy nor my mothers.

> Mango man is also a strange creature,
> He fails to judge those who make them toys.
> From decades divide and rule is most suitable culture,
> Different dwellers dwell delimiting different deity
> deploys.

My mother feels unsafe in my company,
After all her old age with me is not insured.
Whom does she love most and stays in whose company,
It is willingness or compulsion, it's never sured.

    I wear new cloths at the time of marriage,
    I am granted warm welcome for the first time.
    I bear expenses of my spouse's stone age,
    Knowingly for a fixed temporary merry time.

If by mistake a princess falls in love with me,
It becomes an apple of discord for the society.
As if a stray black bumblebee intents to suck queenless bee.
But besides both, bridles bear ban being born from different deity.

    Guests don't like to come to my house,
    How can I adjust them in my small cabin?
    In order to avoid angry relatives' grouse,
    My generations sign a round robin.

Anyway, people don't like to come to me,
What do I have, to give my loved ones?
The world from my point of view, why don't they see?
I am often stuck in critical climax compulsions.

    People think that I only make lame excuses.
    I am not Hanuman who can tear chest and show it.
    When will people finally trust me who abuses?
    On the scale of the world, why do I not fully fit?

If God has gifted the tongue to people,
Has God given them right to speak anything?
Am I born to hear only abuses of the people?
Or insult is something better than nothing?

> For the world I am the cheapest of goods,
> But for my family, I am their world.
> Poor's world has neither security nor foods,
> How can God create such a biased world?

After all, poors' world is too created by God,
Then why so much injustice to these poor people.
God is nearer but beyond reach is earthly lord,
I blow bootless bells in the temple of justice's steeple.

> What is the logic behind hell creation?
> Is it a punishment for the sins of my previous birth?
> Or it is the way of my purification for salvation,
> Why I am not allowed to enter into heavenly earth?

I need leisure time to gaze beautiful earth,
But goal is vague whether it is of short run or long run.
As I have been in the red since birth,
I am afraid as time and tide waits for none.

> I ought to be drummed out of army,
> But still bravely prepare to face the music.
> Defeated disgusted defender never feels palmy,
> As only intrinsic pleasure paves joy extrinsic.

I chatter over flooded murmuring pond,
Water roars like heart of vices.
Frogs croak with mysterious sound,
I bubble hearing confused babbles of voices.

    One day Mango man would rule,
    Birds would chirp melodiously day and night.
    One day falcon would deny being falconer's tool,
    And mango man would be crowned for right.

Now it's time to unite ourselves,
We should try to ignite one another.
Aside alienation from our true selves,
All deprived needs assistance as brother.

    Think, we are still a malleable mango,
    Mango of premium class.
    Engulfed farmers need firm flow,
    Otherwise be ready for loss, be ready for loss.

I am dearest son of God,
And father always stands with his son.
My grievances may be with earthly lord,
But I have inherited this as a son.

    Tamed soul would be freed one day,
    Tamed soul would rule over the world.
    Freedom of pigeons would be welcomed one day,
    Exploitation would be finished from the world.

The day is not too far,
When disparities would be finished for fated.
And there would not be a single bar,
In God's eyes whenever it would be rated.

I am deeply rooted mango man,
Not an easy task to uproot my ground.
Even super natural elements would be my fan,
And God would grace me with his sound.

One day Goddess Saraswati would enlighten us,
Darked dark nights would pass forever.
Who do dare to derail or crush saints?
Whom Goddess Durga is the Saver?

Maa Saraswati is the Goddess of wisdom,
Maa Luxmi is the Goddess of wealth,
Mango Man prays them all for his stardom,
May Maa Durga would give mango men such
strength! Such strength! Such strength!

BY: -   SATISH ANAND

Part:-2(Mangoism)

Collectivism focuses on the group for supremacy,
While lotus like individuals flourish individualism.
Thorn like mango man can beautify rose like democracy,
Mango man centered democracy designs juicy Mangoism.

I am a newly born mango breed leader,
My leadership is of my own choices.
My house is made of straw and feather,
Where different doers dwells in duel guises.

Democracy is for people,
But for people of puppet size.
Insects march in a row like creeper,
But rulers rowdyism is of elephant size.

Poor mob is marching behind,
Aware gets their part of hay
Unaware are getting blind and blind,
Trees shed tears in the May.

We are born free,
But always in chains.
We can see tall tree,
But eyes full of dry rains.

Democracy is known for freedom of people,
But freedom is only for elite class.
People's government governed by people,
But people's heart is like a broken glass.

Divided deserves dictatorial democracy,
Illiterate Indians ideate ignited India insanely.
Leprous leaders lead long lasted leprosy,
Our offsprings obey ordinary ordains only.

Mango man has been passing days in destitute,
Even God is too much cruel to him.
Helpless housewife is forced to prostitute,
In cloudy sky stars sink dim.

Democracy is the form of government,
Government is of the people, for the people, by the people.
If the public is ignorant, then whose reflection is the
government?
In such a situation, the election is just murder of bodies triple.

What type of parliament do we have?
Disfigured bodies can be seen in mirror or parliament,
Why are culprits imposed on us to save?
How can a bulb blink without filament?

My childhood passes without learning,
No one guides me in proper manner.
My adulthood is busy in earning.
I am sturdy steel, my head hits hammer.

Education is no one's priority,
Whosoever demands for wits?
Educated voters are in minority,
To unfurl flag, straight flag staff fits.

I am a product of Stone Age,
My network never gets any signal.
I can't pay tax, even I can't bear brokerage,
Government has considered me void and null.

The world is created for me,
The world is very beautiful.
The government is formed for me,
The government is largely dutiful.

The police are employed for my security,
But police are never honest to me.
The court is created for my justice,
But court is the costliest affair for me.

Free education is meant for me,
Schools are opened to spare my time.
Atmosphere is polluted, but there is no tree,
Is a child responsible, or is it a political crime?

Government hospitals are running without fuel,
As if there is no difference between life and death.
How can deoxygenated bodies challenge oxygenated for duel,
If there is a big bias between air quality which they breath?

All higher posts and jobs are reserved for convent educated,
Who are elite and products of private sectors.
If private sector opts convent educated,
Why not government seats are reserved for products of
public sectors.

Either education or health, I am far lagging behind,
But competition is going on at the same track.
Has our system gone blind,
Poor mountaineer is flagged without back?

Who is interested in joining rallies?
Unaware unemployed only adds gathering.
Starvation stays empty bellies,
Hoping for wellness, life is weathering.

My all efforts end in smoke,
Scarcity is a part and parcel of my life.
Poverty stricken stage is easy to provoke,
Conflict of mind adds extra strife.

A light purse is a heavy curse,
Poverty instigate people for violence.
Sufferers of injustice, who can nurse?
Equal opportunity paves the path of non-violence.

Corruption exists in full swing,
My opportunities are swallowed by dragon.
I am hopeful from a hollow ring,
Knowing that our leaders are enjoying foreign wagon.

Some people invest their money,
Some people invest their time.
Political chair only comments funny,
Life is left unheard, without rime.

Prevention is better than cure,
As an open door tempts even a saint.
Better to sweep before your own door,
One who preaches only, easily faint.

Some people are born to be used,
Mean masters use and throw.
Unwanted guests come to be abused,
Vain mornings begin with musical crow.

Weak bricks build weak building,
Frail items faint easily.
Everything needs capacity building,
To keep outdated items is very silly.

Easy to rule over donkeys,
Horse may make fall his rider.
Moron mob is like mute monkeys,
Whose thought is narrow, can never be wider?

It is a big conspiracy,
To make me wander in the dark nights.
Sad streaming sound is my legacy,
But everyone knows, barking dogs seldom bites.

One must lay up something for a rainy day,
Preparation in advance is the part of bravery.
Wise servants may be masters one day,
But who would kindle the flame to finish their slavery?

If constitution bases both poor and rich,
Why so many acts needed to constitute?
If everyone has to bowl on same pitch,
Then why does pauperism push one to substitute?

A closed mouth catches no fly,
Success comes by smart work only.
Doing own work, why should I shy?
Far from realities, gets jerks only.

I am a distressed devotee,
My devotion disappears with distress.
Occasionally, God is lied and paid fee,
Leads the desirous devotion to a mess.

My little valuables now demonetized,
Their hush money to be whitewashed.
Fake politicians must be monetized,
Why do my feelings harassed and grassed?

I am in queue for a little money,
Bankers provide them home service.
My baby cries for a penny,
In their own court they play tennis.

Job is in danger, bread is missing,
Big debate is going on, media smiles.
Government expenses, corruption, debtors are hissing,
Is country rising only in fake files?

Everyone pretends to be my well wisher,
Then, why am I always cursed?
No one is looking cheater,
Manifesto wounds are always nursed.

Night seems deep dark doom,
My morning is missing at Moon.
Fog and mist are in boom,
End is now approaching soon.

Cashless is not only a digital fight,
But who deserves decisions, where and when to start.
Is political funding only white,
Of which rallies and elections are deciding part?

Patriotic preachers preach only for others,
Their attitude and motive is usually lamed.
Examples and suggestions are set for us,
We commoners are only to be blamed.

Black money backs politicians,
It's a ladder to come in power.
Honest honey tongues are magicians,
Millions of rupees they get from shower.

I walk miles to earn my hay,
They walk miles to digest butter.
Society respects civilized gay,
Complete mango man lives in gutter.

My life is always dramatized,
I clap for my mockery.
Victory of mine is customized,
Is it a theatre or producers robbery?

I am a complex number,
Election makes me countable.
Formed government deeply rests in slumber,
As knowing my bitterness is non durable.

Is it cold blooded murder of democracy?
Or is it mockery of a common man?
Is it beginning of rude aristocracy,
Or is it latent legal liberty ban?

I have the gift of the gab,
I am able to sway the mob.
My ability is cut by politician's nab,
They are experts in authorizing rob.

I don't want to be a big draw,
But I deserve a little bit respect.
Strongers' survival is the nature's law,
"Existence ends exploitation" is only a filmy fact.

I am a lean and mean sheep,
I march with my flock.
But my connectivity is not so deep,
Anyone can open this keyless lock.

I am a blind follower,
I know to march in a row.
We don't need any whistle blower,
Without arrow, why do we need bow?

Intellectuals are as quiet as the grave,
Media is as black as it is painted.
Nation's soul is in prison, nothing to save,
Constitutional bodies are badly dented.

I am known as smallest retailer,
Even multi-millionaires are allowed to sell green balls.
My brothers are left for me as bargainer,
Having paying capacity are welcomed in the malls.

I grow goods for my own creepers,
But no one is ready to water it.
I am badly challenged to escape from grippers,
After all big traders do a favor to make my produce fit.

I have become a beneficiary victim of bread democracy,
Even I have to sell my ancestral assets to feed my body.
My small shop has been gulped by big bosses' policy,
As retail business is opened for foreigners by our step daddy.

I am tempted to be a merchant of joy,
I own tears by expending diamonds.
Big bulls bump economy freely like a toy,
Whereas small traders are bounded with the bonds.

"The Survival of the fittest" is the ageless law of nature,
One sun shines to engulf millions of stars.
Powerful creature depends on weak creature,
Only one king celebrates with few survivors after wars.

Some people are born only to be fodder for others,
When is their life or death recorded in history?
They have neither family nor brothers,
Do their wounds know defeat or victory?

Democracy is as simple as cow,
Starved to death still ready to feed.
Politicians pose pretending mow,
Tied with pillars waits for weed.

Public is as green as grass,
But politicians are as dead as mutton.
Pure gold is layered with base brass,
Whereas manifesto burns with the pressing of button.

Awareness is the greatest need of hour,
Even extent of exploitation causes crucial fights.
Puppet size public chooses kings like tower,
Whereas they have been begging for equal rights.

Our constitution guarantees equal rights all rounds,
Since centuries haves and have-nots having different poles.
Whenever a clarion call to political wakefulness sounds,
Same greatest book shows to riches different holes.

Slavery is going great guns,
But shouts of liberty sound only in soul.
Dreams are nightmares having funs,
Own shoes pinches with hollow sole.

Democracy is formed in kingly way,
And freedom is dying by inches-inches.
King may keep mob a million miles away,
But wearer knows where the shoe pinches.

Our constitution is as clear as crystal,
Even legislature is as busy as a bee.
In sunny dark day super stars twinkle,
Singing songs of thou thy thee.

Executive is as cheap as dirt,
Judiciary is as blind as a bat.
Honesty guises with genuine flirt,
Now, who is going to bell the cat?

Everybody believes might is right,
Very few feels rights raise responsibilities.
Responsibilities pass through plight,
And plight pledges pure abilities.

One should beware of grave guy,
One who sheds crocodile tears?
Once bitten twice shy,
But emotional blackmailer never fears.

"Like public, like king" symbolizes and mirrors any democracy,
A one-eyed man is crowned amongst blind men.
Political world is full of pretense, deceit and hypocrisy,
Only then political mirage honestly cheats millions of
mango men.

Politics is as cold as charity,
Politicians are as gay as a lark.
Voters always reveal something fishy,
Still frail fishes cast vote for shark.

I am a queer fish,
Usually I lock horns with shark.
Sharks welcome delicious dish,
But coward dogs are meant to bark.

House is as old as the hills,
Whereas residents are as light as feather.
Shark breaths with millions of gills,
But fishes have to face the toughest weather.

Our democracy is new naive in air,
Organs are not yet fully developed.
Our politicians are too knave to care,
Under organ trafficking welfare is enveloped.

My wants and wishes are unlimited,
Knowingly unknowingly I dig my own grave.
My desires fix with my own leaders limited,
I forget they come through same crave.

Above the line resources are unlimited,
Representatives are ready to be sold.
Have-nots are consoled for resources being limited,
Slavery in minds never let them bold.

Bureaucracy is as timid as a mouse,
History witnesses corporate conspires for power sharing.
Ministers are trapped under gorgeous blouse,
Whereas house keepers are never caring.

Bull moves wearing face bearish,
And bear appears with bull's mask.
Liver of commons is having disorder liverish,
Bad health of economy is corporates' task.

Corporate hires county,
County follows poor politicians.
Politicians show beautiful bounty,
Bountiful mob is fascinated by mean magicians.

Market is meant to confuse Commons only,
Corporate world decides directions of stars.
Small traders are for adding adversity adversely,
Multi millionaires are sufficient for giving scars.
Government sector is meant for welfare,

But privatization is going on rapidly.
If everything is controlled, who is freed from flexi fare?
Why our earth, air, water and sky are sold freely.

The corporate is established for my employment,
Is the corporate non-profit religious organization?
If the corporate has right only as tapping claimant,
Why is there no permanent job security at my station?

Do only the corporate contribute in the economy?
Why they deserve complete commands over resources.
Funded parties claim country not more than their colony,
Brokers yell as if direct taxes are their only sources.

Is petroleum necessary goods?
Is everything transportable through water?
Do I not eat or drink living in woods?
Why are heavy indirect taxes not a debatable matter?

Who are the owners of these sectors?
What are the motives of these parties?
Why do paid media support traitors?
Who is behind curtain these adoptees?

Nothing is essential; nothing is tax free for me.
Still I am a culprit of taking unnecessary grants,
Group of gangs united together around queen bee,
All sister concerns are ready and rants.

I don't need unnecessary subsidy or charity at alms,
I just want equal opportunity to move forward.
Who gives me scars usually moves with balms,
It's just a conspiracy to keep me backward.

The world wants me as a cheap labourer,
They want to win by riding on my back.
How can they lose their saviour?
It's just like hard nut to crack.

Corporate clique bounces by leaps and bounds,
East India flourishes by fair means or foul.
Kings cling traitors making rounds over rounds,
Foreign falcon kills only domestic fowl.

Puppet politicians play puppet show in public,
Commons stand in a row and clap.
Paid media is ready to click click click,
Constitutional bodies are only to play in the lap.

If I am not empowered to fight,
Then am I only entitled to an apology?
Issue is not about, who is wrong, who is right?
The aim is just to trap me in tricky terminology.

Is this a characteristic of a public welfare state?
People are looted in the name of public welfare.
What state we desire for, what is our state,
Wherever we woo, well being is wounded by fare.

Are holy rivers blessed only for being impure?
Is it not necessary to clean the minds before cleaning
rivers?
Like sea our rivers can be filled with precious pearls pure,
After all our political system have multi talented divers.

Time is witness; the easiest way to fool is to win faith,
Even a learned person gets caught in the web of illusion.
Leaders lead even those who don't believe in myth or
wraith?
When mind is constrained, nothing seems real or
delusion.

How long will the courtiers immersed in the joy of
nymphs?
What do the inhabitants of heaven know about hellish
life?
For how long will the bloods of mobs pass through
veinless lymphs?
Is modern democracy still traditional monarchy's wife?

Why should the residents of heaven have the special
right?
Who are they to have responsibilities of improving hellish
life?
If all the luxuries exhausted among kings and courtiers'
fight,
Then who should be penalised for commoners' strife?

After all, this practice has been going on since centuries,
Since centuries the poor have been treated like beasts.
How would deep wounds fade away from our memories?
Authoritarian government is that a guardian of law
usually cheats.

Mango man must raise voice for Mangoism,
Struggle for "Mangoism" enlightens Mango Mind.
Mangoism seeks merits of both Collectivism and Individualism,
"Mangoism" portrays plight of political poorly blind.

One cannot have such a realisation of the political dearth,
That one can critically think or copy.
There are more things in heaven and earth,
Than are dreamt of in our philosophy.

There are no slaves in the God's kingdom,
But freedom has been seized by some devils' slaves.
Only those who are once slaves feel the joy of freedom,
Can the cost of freedom be declared so cheap by knaves?

There is no room for doubt or bet,
Freedom is badly misused for political movement.
The seeds of freedom have not even been sprouted yet,
Is there no room for any improvement?

Some politicians preach hate speech in public,
There should be a strict law against it.
What type of democracy it is, what type of republic?
Does extra flexibility of constitution anywhere fit?

Modern politicians fire at the speed of latest missiles,
Is politics a business or service having code of ethics?
'Sovereign Socialist Secular Democratic Republic', is still a
far cry in files,
Is there any other profitable business like politics?

A pushy leader squanders country's assets,
A reckless planner answers with arrogance.
In their mindset sun never sets,
Is public money meant for extravagance?

Baseless base can't walk without walker,
Is chair so lame that needs either money or muscles back?
It is not a business of persuasive talker or honest hawker,
Finding a poor politician is as easy as finding a needle in a
haystack.

Proud of power is like a poisonous tree,
It grows inside like groundless root.
An intoxicated mind never gets free,
Whosoever tastes its flower or fruit?

The leaves are dancing on the ground,
The bees are humming, the snakes are hissing.
Who is the prey, who is the hound?
Media is buzzing, big whales are fishing.

Time clock tick tocks, debates are going on,
Politicians try to put the clock of progress back by
inducting disputes.
Debaters try to put the cart before the horse to egg on,
The master mind creates mirage thinking others as brutes.

Collectivism focuses on the group,
While individualism focuses on the individual.
Too many birds together neither sings nor scroop,
While single bird's state seems secluded without visual.

Collectivist ignores individuals when one talks:
Power should be in the hands of the people as a whole,
Not in the hands of a few powerful folks.
But how does state flourish without individual's goal.

Individualism stresses the needs of the individual,
Over the needs of the group as a whole.
Ideally, in a collectivist society, decisions benefit all the
people.
If state is a necessary evil then an individual is whose
soul?

Not a single theory having one side,
Even Collectivism is the opposite of Individualism.
Each and every theory, something they show, something
they hide,
"Mango Man" needs nothing less than "Mangoism".

I am just like a special new breed,
Not a single ism suits for me.
Right to respectful life is my only greed,
A modified old ism is my enlightment's key.

I am badly crushed, exploited and perished political
Mango Man,
The situation for which this system is responsible, I don't
want such an ism.
Why shouldn't the Governance be such, where progress
everyone can,
I will never be satisfied with less than Mangoism...
Mangoism... Mangoism...

BY: -   SATISH ANAND

Part:-3(Mango Mind)

God! O God! One day "Mango Man" would win your
confidence!
You are almighty, omnipresent, omniscient and kind to
your sons,
God! O God! One day Mango Man's cottage would be
your residence!
Your blessings bring good health, wealth, name, fame, and
fortune in tons.

I am a mango man, I am diamond, and I am blessed,
I thank God for each moment and everything that
happens to me.
I am a common man, I am unique, and I am blessed,
I feel gratitude for each moment and everything that
happens for me.

Misfortune is followed by Good fortune,
The God takes away, and then God gives away.
Good fortune is followed by misfortune,
The God gives, and the God takes away.

There is nothing like permanent,
God examines his sons time to time.
Nature changes moment to moment,
Nothing is commoner, nothing is prime.

Time is precious than gold,
It doesn't allow buyback offer.
Life and death no one can hold,
Who postpone every work on tomorrow, they only suffer.

Excess of everything is bad except Learning,
Limitless learning leads to open the door of Heaven.
Everything diminishes after division except learning,
"Mango Mind" drives away enemies like nine two eleven.

Politics is an integral part of all social being,
What the hell this politics is! Nothing here is fun.
Mango mind motivates all, Mango Man is fleeing,
But "Mango Polity" takes cowardly decisions to cut and run.

Mind develops with the accumulation of experiences,
But a little learning is a dangerous thing.
Excess of learning makes differences,
So, drink deep in the Pierian Spring.

Mango man needs love and mental strengths,
Is society not meant to socialize all first?
Love is natural, in love anyone can go to any lengths,
But law is not sufficient to quench anyone's thirst.

I am all oak and iron bound,
I perspire a lot to earn some money.
Hard work is as sound as a pound,
That pushes me ahead in my journey.

Winners never excuses,
Losers always have.
Fuse wire neither explodes nor defuses,
Because blame can only be borne by brave.

Fame is winners reward,
Whereas insult is losers pick.
Appreciation even turns a lagger forward,
But dejection damps down a fire very quick.

Traveler rests under scented shade,
But who do feel gratitude for cute creation?
Lives that feed us, the leaves that fade,
Disrespect them all is violation of natural resolution.

Hands that feed us, the heart that pawn,
Searches our eyes every day, from dawn to dusk.
Dreams every night from dusk to dawn,
Deers are like humans having musk.

An empty vessel makes much noise,
I am as sound as a barrel now.
Dependency on medicines is never wise,
I have faith over sacred cow.

Success and failures are two sides of the same coin,
Success gives much pleasure lesson less.
With each episode of failure some lessons join,
Hence failure paves the path for success.

Each and every theory is favorable-unfavorable,
Have you seen a coin of single side?
Ones mindset makes one able or disable,
Each and every challenge hides opportunity inside.

A happy mind finds happiness at every corner,
Sadist searches sorrow among sweetest sounds.
Mother feeds later but baby cries earlier,
Not a single place where happiness or sorrow not arounds.

Hell and heaven exists only on the earth,
It all depends how one feels.
Someone feels contented, someone feels dearth,
Only outlook of ones forms faded food or tasty meals.

If success holds a grudge into head,
Keeps next success far apart.
Habitual failure makes one depressed,
If failure stays longer in the heart.

Success never comes alone,
New relatives form with name and fame.
Failure forces to listen impolite tone,
Best lessons are linked with near ones blame.

Pessimists regret for what has passed,
Optimists gird up their loins for the future.
It's mindset that moulds one into happy or harassed,
Positivity needs to be adopted for successful culture.

Practice makes a man perfect,
Winners never lose heart till success.
Wisdom guides to accept the fact,
Losers lead the ladder of success.

Braves never taste the defeat deliciously,
Cowards have habits to cry over spilt milk.
Millions of silkworms contribute tirelessly,
It 's how the world gets genuine golden silk.

Where there is a will,
There is a way.
Where there is a hill,
There is a bay.

A sea change is required to change the system,
Braves never leave everything on cruel fate.
Body parts are weak, but constitution a strong stem,
Let's start, as "Good things come to those who wait."

Handsome is that handsome does,
One should remember haste makes wastes.
Politics must pave peaceful path without grudge,
Suggestions to monkeys cost own nests.

If someone is too big for their boots,
They are nearer the church farther from heavens.
An oak flourishes having deep roots,
Gripped grass root work aids at sixes and sevens.

Excess of everything is bad,
Beauty knows that beauty has wings.
Extra expectations engrave someone sad,
Suffocated spirit single song sings.

Precaution is better than cure,
"Good mind, good find" is well known.
Peaceful mind guarantees success sure,
Furious mind is meant only to moan.

Everyone knows unity is strength,
One swallow does not make a summer.
Single strength leaves behind length,
Isolated cell turns into tumor.

Election days are nine days' wonder,
Prejudiced public perception is poor concept.
Mistakes again and again are known as blunder,
One eyed forms government, whom blinds accept.

Finding fault is an easy task,
But finding remedy is the wisest concept.
Politicians tempt with disguised tempting mask,
So self example is better than precept.

A Little knowledge is a dangerous thing,
Bookish knowledge is like a drop in the ocean.
A learning bird soars with simple sober wing,
Intoxicated minds die with wrong notion.

Too much courtesy, too much craft,
But a lie has no legs to stand upon.
Honesty never tussles in any downdraft,
Whereas crafty crook encounters crafty Don.

Experts do the same thing,
But in a different way.
As planets move in a similar ring,
But none gets equal ray.

A job half done is as good as none,
Perfection pours purity at the end.
Jack of all trades is master of none,
Timely updated expertise, one needs to mend.

Books are considered as best friend,
Everyone is ready to betray any time.
Only victorious are rewarded in the end,
Finally any investment on books seems only dime.

Millions make efforts, and millions left behind.
Who remembers those who never wins and easily bend?
For losers, everyone is cruel, no one is kind,
As the world welcomes winners, is the only trend.

Better be alone than in a bad company,
A burnt child dreads the fire.
Millions of bees are dishoused to get honey,
Learning from the world always fire.

Mysterious man minds mindless bashing,
Beware of a wolf in sheep's clothing.
Crows are never the whiter for washing,
So the thought of inferiority fills with loathing.

Pure gold doesn't fear the flame,
A guilty conscience needs no accuser.
Fear stricken impose on others their own blame,
Because they know beggars can't be the chooser.

Love makes a person blind,
A blind man is no judge of colors.
Only rarer shoots in the teeth of the wind,
So, one should be prepared to face temblors.

Child is the father of man,
Like mother, like father, like son and daughter.
Someone enjoys freedom, someone faces ban,
A liege lives like lambs to the slaughter.

Equality exists in the heavenly nature,
Gender differences are rarely expressed.
Law is not enforced to strong creature,
Weaker are meant to be oppressed.

Handsome is that handsome does,
So do good and forget.
Working bees never buzz,
What we did is that what we get.

Proper plans give good result,
Trend says much ado about nothing.
Unsatisfactory result is an insult,
But think something is better than nothing.

Negativity darkens even strong spirit,
Let the past bury its dead.
Time teaches to value each minute,
So that there's no needs to regret on deathbed.

Life is the bed of roses,
Life is not the bed of thorns.
It all depends on what one possess,
Someone picks roses, someone thorns.

Strong stars break in starry sphere,
Adversity reveals "blood is thicker than water".
Best comes out, when worst is there,
Even there is music when rainy tears patter.

There is no pattern of crowd,
Selling cost adds great cry little wool.
Big brands boast of feeling proud,
Simple attitude makes us cool.

Wise hunters keep all arms together,
Better to kill two birds with one stone.
Unwise survives under the weather,
Two dogs fight over a single bone.

An empty brain is a devil's work shop,
Devils gather thistles and expect pickles.
As you sow, so shall you crop,
Many a little makes a mickle.

Hypocrite hermit hunts up God's traces,
Sinner priests rob Peter to pay Paul.
Does real God hide behind religious faces,
Where holy beneficiary shops are able to stay on the ball?

Broker is the king, traders trade,
As the king, so are the subjects.
Whosoever is guilty for poor grade?
When public behaves like objects.

Everyone runs after in cat races,
A bird in hand is worth two in the bush.
Why we forget each coin wears two faces,
Attractive bait digs grave to push.

Company must be fair and square,
One is known by the company one keeps.
Think "why are diamonds forever and rare?"
Prophet pays timely while progress peeps.

A guilty mind is always suspicious,
Where there is fire, there is smoke.
Purity doesn't hide behind dubious,
Empty vessel makes much noise and croak.

Every hobby of the world is not nurtured,
Neither glass toys are to be tossed.
Some wishes may be fulfilled or cultured,
But not every wish is to be postponed to God.

Everyone has a wish in his dream world,
Everyone has some desires in the heart.
If they are fulfilled then God exists in the world.
Otherwise God too is infidel and meant to hurt.

Winners never excuses, losers always have,
As we know "Where there is a will, there is a way".
Mountains only can face strong wave,
Success demands continuous efforts night and day.

God grants grace to those who are as hard as nails,
Goddess guides and give them boon.
Destiny damns those who curses fate and wails,
God ignores those who appear once in a blue Moon.

A light purse makes a heavy heart,
A friend in need is a friend indeed.
A heavy purse makes a light heart,
Books are best friend whosoever read.

Toughest journey is a blessing in disguise,
Immunity seems stronger than royal kings.
Traitors hide under the patriot's guise,
Cuckoo tongue-tied if scroop sound sings.

Peaceful world seems sweeter in cloudy night,
In sunny days star doesn't guise.
Barking dogs seldom bite,
As actinic actor doesn't noise.

By trying the Greeks got into Troy,
There's no rose without a thorn.
As we know, no joy without alloy,
Defeat after defeat winner is born.

What we have is that, what we distribute,
Happy distributes happiness.
When man loses heart, gods execute,
But sad person spreads sadness.

Little pleasure makes toads cry,
More you desire, more you sad.
Everything is yellow to the jaundiced eye,
Excess of everything is bad.

A wolf may lose its teeth,
But not nature.
Something can be modified a little bit,
Halo glimpses from nature and signature.

As far as personality is concerned,
The halo represents holiness or sanctity.
Morning shows the days discerned,
Mindset decides either devil or deity.

Don't put too much iron in the fire,
You can't always get what you want.
Overambitious always keeps starry desire,
Everyone gets what gods grant.

God knocks the door, destiny clatter,
Motivation maps mope's minds little bit.
One can lead an unfortunate horse to water,
But no one can make him drink it.

God helps those who help themselves,
God is the genuine judge of our deeds.
One who blames gods is destiny's slaves,
Blaming birds behaves as futile weeds.

Everyone plays their roles as God's toy,
He whom God steers sails safely.
To whom the gods wish to destroy,
He first makes them mad sanely.

Rome was not built in a day,
Even extreme blessings base the deepest desire.
Consistent efforts are required not for a day,
After all indomitable spirit no one can hire.

It is not an easy task, hard nut to crack,
As life is a riddle, success is not easily met.
In the beginning, the world whom calls freak,
Later the same world declares them great.

Faith over God can move mountains,
But God gives opportunities that can fire.
Ideal fuel heats easily and ignition attains,
So where there's smoke, there's fire.

Great personalities are like ideal fuels,
They burn themselves to enlighten others.
Success and failure always have duels,
As fire and smoke are twin brothers.

Dearest sons deserves most difficult tasks,
Major challenges work like smoke.
In difficulty a wolf in lamb's clothing unmasks,
Honest hard work with faith ignites good stroke.

More you struggle, more you get,
There is no substitute to hard work.
Shortcuts to success, usually traps you in the net,
Only God's court has strongest network.

God fearing bird never hurts anyone,
Faith over goodness is their strength.
No one can harm to God gifted son,
Whose heart is filled with kindness at length.

It doesn't matter how it appears,
Matter is that what is hidden inside.
Strong wings fly high without fears,
Skilled sailors never afraid of high tide.

The man who moves the mountain,
Begins by executing easy targets.
One who dives under learning fountain,
What he desires, what he gets.

Laziness is the greatest enemy inside,
They believe "Early to bed, late to rise."
Passive player sets fixed plan aside,
Idleness makes us unhealthy, pauper and unwise.

The early bird gets the worm,
A good beginning almost assures success.
Late riser loses in the storm,
The threat of imminent Holocaust, no one can guess.

Time is money,
Money breeds time.
Bumblebees enjoy honey,
Buzzing bees create melodious rhyme.

One shouldn't talk about the hind legs of a donkey,
Actions must speak louder than words.
There is no use to be such a cheeky monkey,
Avoid living in a monkey see, monkey do worlds.

Don't put all your eggs in one basket,
A single strike can ruin your entire dream.
Broken dreams can't be purchased from market,
Exhausted energy makes candescent light dim.

There is no place like home,
East or West, home is the best.
Our body requires grass, not foam,
House becomes home with trough and crest.

People who live in glass houses,
Lives in the grip of fear.
Threatening teems thrown stone pauses,
Even surrendered sounds no one hear.

Man never fights with man,
Ego collides with ego.
Two mentals are required, not a single can,
Quarrelsome enjoys bite like mosquito.

To oppose someone powerful is a difficult task,
Revolutionaries only need to get their ducks in a row.
Braves never hide behind the mask,
Cowards are afraid of their own shadow.

Morals alone can't make house strong,
It is essential to lead life like glass.
Transparency is also not wrong,
But too much simplicity is only to harass.

Who does bite the hand that feeds?
Feelings of gratitude unite heart.
Who does cut the tree that seeds?
Closer the stabber, deeper the hurt.

A thick grey cloud may mask the sun for a while,
But stars never hide for too long.
Optimists are always ready to go an extra mile,
Pessimists waste time by singing same song.

Start with confidence makes one rich,
Winners readily hope for the best.
Over confidence may queer the pitch,
So losers need to prepare for the worst.

Reality is fleeting,
Appearances are deceptive.
Hypocrisy is fleeting,
But young generation is receptive.

Beauty is only skin deep,
Don't judge a book by its cover.
Inner face keeps real keep,
Denatured nature loves natural lover.

The pen is mightier than the sword,
The elevator doesn't go to the top floor.
Knowledge is the only earthly lord,
Success needs a foot in the learning door.

Slaves work over, what they don't have,
The grass is always greener on the other side.
One should know, Time never waits for slave,
Mistakes of the past are only future's guide.

Braves accept challenges readily,
Fortune only favors the bold.
Creep mouse fires easily,
But elephant lives like cold.

Too many cooks spoil the food,
Many men possess many minds.
Negative mindset never thinks good,
Whereas good minds, good finds.

Uncivilized society never feels,
Quarrelsome nature is their inbuilt fact.
Who does win in the duel of wheels?
Where there is nothing stays intact.

Unity is strength,
A gram cannot break the furnace.
Isolation keeps success at arm's length,
But the drum sounds better at a distance.

Truth is always bitter,
But evil can't thrive forever.
Honesty is gold that not easily glitter,
Too late to mend, it is never.

On the way we counter many stations,
An open door tempts even a saint.
Evil pursuits bring evil reputations,
If fallen from eyes, who can paint?

A bad man is better than bad name,
But good name is better than gold.
Although destiny declares name and fame,
But hard work is always paid never cajoled.

Sometimes life faces unexpected bounce,
But where there are mountains, there are ditches.
Challenges looks like a vulture waiting to pounce,
But a bouncer bounces easily on unfair pitches.

Successful persons prepare their own ground,
They practice hard at different pitches.
Impossible seems possible when regular efforts sound,
Still challenges give opportunities on unfair pitches.

A robber in the grab of a saint,
Shatters the faith of millions of devotees.
Some selfish enters only to dent,
Money is their religion, are their deities.

The obvious needs no evidence,
Lions never mew, they only roar.
Braves never measure sky's fence,
Coming events cast their shadows before.

Misfortune spoils the mind,
Words and deeds differ of a bad person.
Having good mind gets good kind,
Attitude differs person to person.

Optimist makes a fortune by hard works,
Pessimists make a mess of everything's.
Genuine mindset never gets jerks,
Whereas fair weather friends are seasonal earthlings.

Work hard, rests all up to gods,
Once plotted cannot be blotted.
Be honest and beware of frauds,
What we get, what has been plotted.

World's wisdoms goes waste on walls,
Where slogans or sayings are of no use.
Mind gets insane when body forces for falls,
Like learning after mistakes mend mind's fuse.

Conspiracy is not hatched in a single day,
Crush them in the beginning who conspire.
One who ignores in the beginning has to pay,
Has anyone ever seen smoke without fire?

Where there is a hope, there is a space,
A drowning man catches at a straw.
Even life exists between a rock and a hard place,
A mountain never flows like a straw.

The darkest hour is just before the dawn,
There's a fixed time and a place for everything.
You would get fruit only if you have sown,
As dark hour ends with the new morning.

No doubt adversity kills intelligence,
Silly jumps out of the frying pan into the fire.
Extraordinary task needs extraordinary patience,
As God gives tasks to energize, not to tire.

Rude people don't value mild language,
As we know rod is the logic of fools.
Donkeys are only meant for carrying luggage,
Sanely some people are born to be used as tools.

Unfortunate never welcomes goddess,
Their black has no other hue.
Suggestions to them are like crying in wilderness,
Mindless mind never respects any clue.

As we know idle hands are devil's workshop,
One rotten fish pollute the whole pond.
So stay stable is better than drop,
Silence is silver, but diamond is to positively respond.

Money talks when the cat gets your tongue,
As we know money is the root of all evils.
Even the oldest of old opts energy of a dynamic young,
After all, money power is backed by the minds of devils.

Talk of the devil,
He is sure to appear.
Evil begets evil,
And angel sure to disappear.

One should be bewared of honey tongue,
A honey tongue is a heart of gall.
One should Keep an arms distance from money tongue,
A money tongue is a mind of extreme small.

There is safety in numbers,
One should put two and two together before decision.
Many hands roll a couple of bombers,
Is freedom not so sweet for every pigeon?

Let bygone, be bygone,
Deciduous plants shed leaves in autumn season.
Wise chews the meat and spits out the bones,
Is crying over spilt milk justified, or has no silly reason?

Do good and cast into the river,
A hidden gift is icing on the cake.
Donations show heart, but secrecy is large liver,
Believe, gods grant more than what they take.

What does a monkey know?
Guzzlers know the taste of a ginger.
Trees on the motherland, like patriotism grow,
Foreigners feel patriots being stranger.

Winners never excuses, losers always have,
A bad workman usually quarrels with his tools.
Losers always loses, what they have,
But still who can teach in the kingdom of fools?

Body doesn't need comfort, still we allow rest,
Knowing that hard work is required to maintain the top.
When time and body signals, why not to care as guest,
Lest ready to repent, when birds have eaten the crop.

Facts don't require proof to stand correct.
Usually the thief blames the cops.
Sometimes suspicious sound seems as prime suspect,
Whereas guiltless guy's grave never hops.

A guilty mind is always suspicious,
Suspicion signals sadness with grief.
Evidence usually hides in the eyes of dubious,
Like a speck in the beard of a thief.

There is no end of learning,
Learning is always as cumin in camel's mouth.
Knowledge can be multiplied only by pairing,
As learning transfers from mouth to mouth.

Simplicity is the best ornament,
But one must be cautious in front of a crook.
Nature is temporary not permanent,
So, one must treat thieves by hook or by crook.

Fairy seems fairy in simple garments,
Poor attention seeker adds colors to adorn.
Anyway beauty needs protector, no ornaments,
After all, how long roses are safe without thorn.

Wise utilizes their time, stupids waste,
As if, "Penny wise and pound foolish."
Fickle minds work with feverish haste,
Cool minds decide wisely either bearish or bullish.

Adversity never comes alone,
It comes with opportunity to rise again.
Secure future plainly passes through danger zone,
So fruitful efforts are required again and again.

Drought of resources,
Deprives man for a single draught.
Tussle between unequal forces,
Enables man for only an empty pot.

Opportunity knocks at the door but once,
Wise never misses the chances.
Inheritance warns," Like father like sons".
Yet from present's hard work, future glances.

Be updated as a lifelong learner,
Opportunity needs to discern.
Learning makes more confident earner,
Which stimulates one more to learn.

Under the sun hair can be grayed,
But time can never be cheated.
The truth can be betrayed,
But it can never be defeated.

Dreaming of prosperous life is an accelerator,
Why not we march with the sun.
What is the use of repenting later?
When the damage is already done.

A prejudiced mind can't reveal the reality of life
One who put foot in others, only become alienated.
Not an easy task to cut the air with a knife,
Better to be alone rather than being humiliated.

Murderer never survives for long,
Diamond cuts diamond very fast,
Evil takes always side wrong,
Only "Do good, have good" longs last.

Ill got ill spent,
As we know, "No pain, no gain".
Stories left behind only to repent,
So let by-gone, be by gone.

Life lends limited life, as death is sured,
God is inside but faith runs after pope.
What cannot be cured, Must be endured,
As long as there is life, there is hope.

Open heart, open body, open brain, open life I have,
No heart problem, no body problem, no brain problem, life
has no problem.
Closed outlook, closed world, closed mindset, closed life I
have,
But body is awesome, brain and heart are awesome, even
my life is awesome.

Time is the greatest reaper; time is the greatest healer,
So be bold, be strong, it is the need of hour.
Time is a vector quantity, time is never scalar,
So, be wise, be genius, smartness is the need of hour.

Stars never shine in the Blue,
Nature teaches us rise and fall.
Old passes away to give space to new,
Permanent is nothing either big or small.

Blaming birds blame God and live mouth from hand,
One should remember one rises only after dip.
Determined will power is essential to stand,
Without ambitions, life is without radar ship.

Full moon succeeds tides over Tides,
Before tsunami still stream flows.
Through high mountains cool west wind rides,
After strong storms fresh breeze blows.

One who is willing to climb to the crest,
Always ready to face those opponents who unitedly try to pull.
Even their strong desire never let them rest.
Success for them is like a red rag to a bull.

The bond of bad people is never strong,
Their dream of doing bad to others is never fulfilled.
Evil forces can't last long,
As the earthen pot of sin gets easily filled.

How bright the sun is,
Is this a new morning!
How bright the future is,
Is this a new beginning?

Mango Man is the symbol of humanity,
Mango Man represents all commons.
Each creation of God has its own sanctity,
Irrespective of caste, color, creed, sex or regions.

Millions of Mango Men, millions of temples we have,
Believe in goodness, Believe in the entity of God.
Goodness to humanity and mankind moves like wave,
God is everywhere; believe in the existence of God.

One must not oppress the poor and weak,
God's son is never alone and helpless.
Remember that breathe of the lifeless blower's beak,
Even can burn strong iron into airy ashes.

God doesn't live only in temples or churches,
The poorest of the poor is omnipresent like God.
Service to humanity and mankind is like diamonds purchases,
One who is more needy, he is more closer to God.

Keep it a secret when you give to the needy,
Why should left hand know, what right hand is doing?
Someone who has an itching palm is always greedy,
Selfless service is required for God's blueing.

God knows everything, nothing is hidden,
Impartial eyes watches, how much we are decent.
From God's eyes and grace no one is forbidden,
So believe in God, God is omniscient.

Maa Saraswati is the Goddess of wisdom,
Maa Luxmi is the Goddess of wealth,
Mango Mind prays them all for his peaceful kingdom,
Maa Durga gives all such strength.

The Earth is rotating regularly,
The Sun rises and sets at right time.
Not a single sphere of the universe is neither late nor early.
Think about that omnipotent that controls this rime.

God inside us, God around us, God exists in each corner
of the world.
Believe "God is the world and the world is God."
Or think, "The world is God, but the God is more than the
world."
In whatever way we serve sons of God, God graces us,
God assists us, and Mango Man is blessed by God...

BY: -   SATISH ANAND

The following poem, ("Quick Fox, Lazy Dog" covers all the sounds of language like all the colors of life whereas next poem, **"Quicker Quacks, Lazy Lacks"** covers each alphabet of the poem **"Quick Fox, Lazy Dog"** and **most lengthy poem of Acrostic style in English Literature**. The poet has employed many poetic devices in the poem and plays with words so beautifully that a lover of literature can find all essential tools that a poet uses to create rhythm, enhance poem's depth meaning, or intensify a mood or feelings of a common man. "Quicker Quacks, Lazy Lacks" also illustrates one root word in different form and **most beautiful poem of Acrostic style ever written in English Literature.)**

4. Quick Fox, Lazy Dog

The quick brown fox jumps,
Over loaded lazy dog dumps.
Laziness is the greatest parasite,
Dire enemy is hidden insider insight.

      Win needs as quick as wink,
      Pomp frail boats mostly sink.
      Idle as gay as a lark,
      Holds life in the dark.

Lazy weaves vampers in mind,
Quicker catches jollity as wind.
Destiny frames no hindrance,
When jubilant warrior joys jubilance.

5. Quicker Quacks, Lazy Lacks

Tearless tears tears tears tearlessly
Hopeless hope hopes hope hopefully,
Echoless echo echoes echoes,

Queenless queendom queens queen.
Unitless unit unites unity.
Issueless issuer issues issues.
Careless carer cares care carelessly
Keyless keylock keys key.

Barest barefaced bares bare barefacedness.
Restless rest rests restlessness restfully.
Offerless offerer offers offerings.
Wantless want wants wants.
Noiseless noisemaker noises noise noisily.

Fearless fear fears fear fearlessly.
Opportunityless opportunist opts inopportune
opportunity.
Xenialxenium xenon's Xenomania.

Jointless joint joins joint jointly.
Useless user uses used user.
Meaningless meaning means mean meaningfulness.
Partless party parts part partly.
Slowest slower slows slows slowly.

Offered offerings offers offer.
Visionless visionary visions visional visions.
Endless end ends end endlessly.
Rootless roots uproot roots roots' rootlessness.

Lamey lame lames lameness.
Optional optant opts optional options.
Aidless aid aids aid.
Daring dare dares darely.
Eased ease eases easily.
Dreamless dreamer dreams dreamland.

Light lighten lights light lightly.
Airless airlines air airy airlifts.
Zooming zoom zooms zoomed zooms.
Yearnless yearning yearns yearn.

Darkless dark darkens dark.
Opinionless opinion opts optional opinions.
Groundless ground grounds grounded ground.

Disabled ability enables enabled abilities.
Utterless utterer utters utterings utterly.
Moneymaker makes moneymaker's money.
Purified impurities impures purification purely.
Sweet sweeter sweetens sweethearts sweetly.

Lifeless life lives lifelong.
Aimless aim aims aimlessly.
Zoomed zoom zooms zoom.

Injurious injurator injures injureless injury.
Noteless notable notes note notably.
Effortless effort efforts effortful efforts.
Soundless sound sounds sound.
Seedless seeder seeds seed.

Impulsive impulse impulses impulsively.
Senseless sensor senses sense senselessly.

Tryluck try tries tries.
Headless header heads header's headache ahead.
Effectless effector effects effectives effectfully.

Grassless grasser grasses grassy grasslands.
Roofless roof roofs roof.
Educationless educator educates educated.
Armless army arms armed army.
Tasteless taster tastes tasty taste tastelessly.
Empathyless empathizer empathizes empathetically.
Shameless shameful shames shamelessly.
Tamed tamers tame tamelessly tamely

Purposeless purpose purposes purpose.
Actless actor acts act actively.
Rhymeless rhymes rhyme rhyme.
Artless artist arts art artlessly.
Staged stager stages unstaged stagings.
Imageless image images imagery images imagelessly.
Toyed toymaker toys toyland,
Escapeless escapist escapes escapades,

Damaged damager damages damages.
Improved improvisator improves improvised
improvements.
Rainless rain rains rainy rain.
Experienced experimentalist experiences experiential
experiences.

Emotionless emotionalist demotions emotionality
emotionlessly.
Needless needy needs need.
Extracted extractor extracts extract extraction.
Moneyless moneylender monetizes moneymakers.
Yeasted yeast yeasts yeastiness.

Inspired inspiration inspires inspirational inspirers.
Shapeless shape shapes shaped shape.

Hidden hide unhides hides.
Impeded impedance impedes impediments.
Dreamy dreamweaver weaves dreamed dreams.
Destined destination destines destiny.
Expanded expansionist expands expansionism.
Non-productive producer produces productive product.

Idealess idea ideates ideas ideally.
Nameless name names named name.
Sleepless sleep sleeps sleeplessly.
Injured injurant injures uninjured injuries.
Deathless death dies deadly.
Exited exit exists exit.
Roasted roaster roasts roasting roasters.

Imprinted imprint imprints imprinting imprints.
Nonuniformed unifier uniforms uniformitarianism.
Sinking sinker sinks sinking.
Invaded invader invades invading invaders.
Greenery-less Greenland greens green greenery.
Highjacked highjackers highjack highjackings.
Tireless tired tires tiring tirelessly.

Wireless wire wires wired wire.
Injected injector injects injections.
Nominated nominator nominates nominations.

Nursed nursery nurses nursing nurseries.
Equal equalizer equalizes equaled equality.
Existing existence exists existed existentially.
Disguised guise guises guised disguisement.
Scarless scar scars scarred scars.

Authorized authority authorizes authoritarian authority.
Sightless sightseeing sights sighted sightlessness.

Questionless questions question questionable
questionnaire.
Unionless union unites unit.
Idealless idealist idealizes idealistic ideals.
Comfortless comfort comforts comfortably.
Knightless knight knights knighthood.

Armourless armourers armours armoured armours.
Speechless speaker speeches speech speechlessly.

Winless win wins win.
Inclined inclination inclines disinclined disinclination.
Natural nature denatures unnatural nature.
Killed killer kills unkilled killings.

Pointless point points pointed point.
Orderly order orders ordered order.
Motherless motherland mothers motherly motherhood.
Powerless powerful powers power's power.

Farmless farmer farms farming.
Reinless rein reins rein.
Ageless aged ages age-long.
Imposed imposer imposes impositions.
Linkless link links linked link.

Bottomless bottom bottoms bottomlands.
Optional option options option optionally.
Actionless action actions actionable action.
Terrorless terrorist terrorizes terrified terrorism.
Spiritless spirit spirits spirituality spiritually.

Mindless mind minds mindful mindlessly.
Oriented orientation orients oriental Orientalism.
Separated separatist separates separation separately.
Talkless talkative talks talking talk.
Legalized illegalities legalize illegals legally.

Yelling yellbluemurderer yells yelled yeller.
Satisfied satisfaction satisfies dissatisfied satisfactorily.
Idiotic idiot idiotizes idiotism idiotically.
Nearby nearers nears nearly nearness.
Knocking knockout knocks knocked knocker.

Inaccurate accuracy accurates accurateness accurately.
Disappeared appearance appears appeared appearance.
Long longings longs longer longingly.
Eyeless eyes eye eyed eyes.

Apartmentless apartment aparts apartments.
Scripted scriptwriter scripts scriptural scriptures.

Guarded guardian guards guardianship.
Argueless argue argues arguments.
Yearning yearn yearns yearned yearn.

Answerless answer answers answerable unanswered.
Shockless shocker shocks shocked shockingly.

Attempering attemper attempers attemperments.

Loveless lover loves lovingly.
Actionless action acts actionable actions.
Relationless relationship relates related relatives.
Keepless keeper keeps keep.

Homeless homer homes homely homeland.
Ownerless owner owns ownership.

Landless landlord lands landed land.
Deedless deed does deed.
Sacrificing sacrificer sacrifices sacrificed sacrifice
sacrificially.

Laughless laughter laughs laughably.
Involved involver involves involvements.
Faceless face faces facebook.
Embryoless embryologist embryos embryo.

Incomplete completion completes completed completer
completely.
Networking networker networks networked networker.

Taught teacher teaches teachless teachings.
Honourless honour honours honourables honourably.
Earthless earth unearths earthly earthlings.

Demonetized monetization monetizes monetized money.
Attemptless attempters attempt attemptable attempts.
Remindless reminder reminds reminded remindings.
Kicked kicker kicks kicking.

Loved lover loves beloved.
Adorable adorer adores adorably.
Zipless zip unzips zipped zipper.
Yellowish yellower yellows yellowed Yellowstone.

Woundless wound wounds wounding.
Enjoyable enjoyment enjoys enjoyment enjoyably.

Addicted addiction addicts unaddicted addictively.
Voteless voters vote votaries.
Entertaining entertainer entertains entertained
entertainments.
Sweetest sweetheart sweetens sweetened sweetness.

Viewless viewer views view.
Attached attachments unattaches attachable attachments.
Mirrorless mirror mirrors mirrored mirroring.
Painless pain pains pains.
Elited elitist elites elitism.
Rhythmless rhythm rhymes rhythmic rhymes
rhythmically.
Shadowless shadow shadows shadowed shadows.

Injured injury injures injuries.
Numberless numbering numbers numbered numberings.

Moveless movement moves movements.
Impure purifier purifies purified purification.
Nonviolent violence violences.
Disclosed disclosure discloses disclosing disclosers.

Quenchless quenching quenches quenched quenchable.
Unbalanced balance balances balanced balance.
Industrious industrialist industrializes industries.
Cropless cropper crops crop.
Kinkless kink kinks kinky kink.
Empowerless empowerment empowers empowered.
Riskless risktaker risks risky risks.

Cashless cashier cashes cash.

Accompanying accompanion accompanies accompanied accompanists.

Thornless thorn thorns thorny thorns.

Cloudless cloud clouds cloudy cloud.

Heirless heir heirs airy heirloom.

Expenseless expenditure expenses expensed expenses expensively.

Scornful scorner scorns scorned scornfully.

Juiceless juicer juices juicy juices.

Outdated dates date dated dates.

Lingering lingerer lingers lingeringly.

Lethal lethargy looses lazybones lethargically

Instigated instigator instigates instigations.

Terrified terrorizer terrorizes terrorizing terror.

Yelped yelp yelps yelping yelp.

Assembled assembly disassembles assembly's assemblers.

Segregated segregation desegregates segregating segregationists.

Wonderful wonderland wonders wonderfully.

Indianized Indian indianizes Indians.

Notified notice notices unnoticed notifications.

Detached attachment attaches attachable attachments.

Disputed disputants dispute disputeless dispute.

Edited editor edits editorial edition.

Sought seeker seeks seekers.

Teamless teammate teams up team's teamwork.
Illegal legitimate legitimizes legitimacy illegitimately.
Nightless night nights night nightfalls nightmares.
Yielded yielder yields yielding yields.

Forceless force enforces forced force.
Repeated repeater repeats repeating repeatables.
Armed army disarms armless army.
Motivated motivator motivates motivationless.
Exceptional exception excepts exceptionable exceptions
unexceptionally.
Solicited solicitor solicits solicitant solicitations.

National denationalization nationalizes nationalized
nationalist.
Occupied occupier occupies occupational occupations.

Handless hand handles handleless handlers.
Impossible possibility possibilidade possible
impossibilities.
Non-conservative conservator conserves conservatives.
Dethroned throne-burn enthrones throne.
Exempted exemplar exempts exemplified exemplification.
Recorded recorder records unrecordable recordings.
Announced announcer announces announcing
announcements.
Nationalized nationalist denationalizes nation nationwide.
Colorless colors colour colorful coloured colors
colorlessly.

Extreme extremist extremes extremists' extremism extremely.
Weedless weed weeds weedy weeds.
Harmless harmful harms harmfully.
Expressionless expression expresses expressed expressions expressively.
Numbered numbers numerate innumerable numbers innumerably.

Jobless jobber jobs job.
Unaddressed addressee addresses addressor.
Backward background backs backing backups.
Irresponsible responsibility responses responsible respondents.
Liked likings likes likeliest likelihood.
Attacked attacker attacks attacking attackers.
Nonsense sense senses senseless sensor.
Tempting temptation tempts tempted.

Warranted warrantee warrants warrantless warranties.
Assessed assessee assesses assessor's assessments.
Requisite requirer requires requisites requisitions.
Regular irregularities regulates irregular regulators.
Irrelevant relevancy relevant relevance.
Objective subjectivity objects objectivism objectively.
Resigned resigner resigns designated resignation.

Joyless joy joys joyful joyfulness joyfully.
Optimistic pessimist optimizes optimistically.
Yoked yokefellow unyokes yokes.
Sold seller sells selling sellouts.

Jokeless joker jokes joked jokes.

Unbearable bearance bears bearable bearings.

Bestowed bestower bestows bestowing bestowal.

Informed informer informs informative informations.

Lovely loveface loves loved lovers.

Ignored ignorant ignores ignorance.

Unadvised advisor advises advisory's advice.

Nailed nailer nails nailers.

Cooked cooker cooks cooking cookery.

Eternal joy provides Jubilance jubilance Jubilance...

BY: - SATISH ANAND

6. Love Leads Life

Be quick like thoughts,
Thoughts paves positivity,
Positivity opens optimistic outlook,
Optimistic outlook rewards quicker,
Quicker person quenches repressesive rivals,
Rivals turn friends,
Friends forms love,
Love leads life,
Life needs struggle,
Struggle seeds success' seed,
Seed germinates success,
Success shapes prosperity,
Prosperity paves peace,
Peace heeds enlightenment,
Enlightenment blesses soul,
Soul loses inside God,
God grants grace,
Grace knows no limit.,
Limit of desires is unlimited,
Unlimited sky covers our universe,
Universe enfolds many galaxies,
Galaxies follow origins,
Origins are like our mothers,
Mothers are the closest goddess,
Goddess never resents from sons,
Sons rarely feel gratitude,

Gratitude goes through greatness,
Greatness never hurts lives,
Lives lead learning,
Learning never ends,
Ends begin from other side,
Side usually wears no face,
Face may disguise mirror,
Mirror never tells lie,
Lie seeks shelter from saints,
Saints shows path of salvation,
Salvation requires selfless service,
Selfless service serves satisfaction,
Satisfaction builds strong personality,
Personality improves with experiences,
Experiences are the crop of time,
Time teaches us to be punctual,
Punctual attains targets timely,
Timely beginning makes us ahead,
Ahead to others adds confidence,
Confidence creates quickness,
Quickness with calm mind creates winners,
Winners only deserve love,
Love teaches to live with love, with love, with love…

BY: - SATISH ANAND

7. Litigation

Taught by my teacher, taught by my friend,
What is democracy, ruler in our hand?

Our parliament is our temple, politicians are devotees,
Poor Indians are assets, but unfair trustees.

Democracy breathes under kingdom impersonation in our nation,
Then what is our aim, what is our destination?

Is it our boon, or is it our bane?
Politicians are corrupted, or public insane.

Is it mockery of our democracy, or is it of court?
Where is our legacy, when motive is short?

Rules and regulations are being wanted by our nation,
But why are these differ for same destination?

RTI is a weapon to get information,
Or is it for accidents, threatening or assassination?

Our country is good, our constitution is the best,
But what for those, who swarm like pest?

Is it our capital, or is it dream land?
River of tears, and houses of the sand.

Nothing to drink, nothing for light,
Is it governance, is it upright?

Freedom we got, but freedom for what?
Surviving for bread, and mobile for chat.

Why someone poor, why someone rich?
When one is our nation, smeared with same pitch.

I am a mango man, my vitality is sucked,
Poison in my mind, my head is ducked.

Promises and responsibilities are my assets, Loans are as gift,
How can I oppose anyone, nothing is to lift?

I am tortured and I am harassed,
I am a soft target, who is always trapped.

Rules and regulations are only meant for us,
Government is our well wisher, is it only fuss?

I am a common man, my memory is weak,
What can we do, when corruption is at its peak?

Is privatization the only way, to uproot corruption?
Or is it politicians' hay, to shoot poors' deduction?

What to do or what to decide?
When everything is open, nothing to hide.

Education system is raped, morality is down,
Students are rapt, but immorality has crown.

If teaching is not a skill, it is a profession,
Teacher is just material, not a builder of nation.

Teacher has to do everything, except teaching,
Is it our education policy, or is it cheating?

All policies are beautiful, but only meant for papers,
Do our policy makers still in diapers?

What type of council, what type of research?
When private publishers flourish, students wander in
search.

Do our education, need certification?
Cheating and forgery are its only essential qualification.

What is Grading system, what is policy of No Detention?
Does it crush competitive outlook, or is it a matter of
contention?

Is it new invention, or is it our modern evaluation?
Grades for faces, not for dedication.

Is it Right to Education or Right to exploit?
Nowhere is dedication, nothing seems right.

Is it justified, or is it just fixation?
Youths are unemployed and retired gets extension.

Is it mockery of energy, or insult of poor sight?
Vote bank to decide, Incandescent or candle light.

If reservation is fair, then why for someone nightmare?
As politicians interfere, deservings are unaware.

What is to disclose, what is to hide?
When everything is illogical, absurd, and mala fide.

Our result is improving, with the rate of crime,
Economy is moving, with the value of dime.

No one thinks for country, no one for nation,
Then where is public interest, where abides civilization?

Some conspires to be sincere; some behave as if bona fide,
Is it volcanic or peace before forthcoming tide?

Honesty is a disease, no medicine can cure,
Isolation is prevention, Death is sure.

I have neither Money, nor legal suggestions,
No one hears excuses, everyone needs our confessions.

Too many suggestions, not a single aid,
Everyone needs cultivation, by making others parade.

I don't know grafting, I don't know drafting,
No one is to help, everyone seems crafting.

So many priests, Temple is only one,
Sacrificer is to be sacrificed, Plea is none.

All around are Beehives, Brokers and agents,
Preach for Justice, and Impersonation is like saints.

Vision for prosperous India, Dream for better Fate,
Try to understand, why I am little Late.

It's not of personal interest, not for name or fame,
It's my essence of life, which makes me lame.

So accept my litigation, in public interest,
Provide us mitigation, to give us rest...To give us rest...To
give us rest.

BY: -   SATISH ANAND